Overwl  By Grace

A Biblical Study of the Grace of God in Salvation

Brian Anderson

To

My Beloved Wife

Debbie

The Finest Woman I Have Ever Known

Contents

~~~~

Page

1. Overwhelmed!..9

2. Our Desperate Need For Sovereign
   Grace...19

3. Electing Grace..35

4. Redeeming Grace: *The Sufficiency of
   the Atonement*..51

5. Redeeming Grace: *The Design of the
   Atonement* 77

6. Redeeming Grace: *The Benefits of the
   Atonement* 93

7. Regenerating Grace.......................................103

8. Preserving Grace..123

9. Questions Concerning Sovereign Grace.......141

10. Responding to Sovereign Grace....................159

Suggestions for Further Reading 165

Chapter 1

Overwhelmed!

Amazing Grace, How sweet the sound
That saved a wretch like me
I once was lost but now am found
Was blind but now I see![1]

John Newton, the author of that world-famous hymn, was born in 1725. By the age of seventeen, he sported one of the worst reputations among the sailors of his day. John filled his days with stealing, lying, and blaspheming. In fact, someone once claimed that John could curse for two hours straight without ever repeating himself! He eventually sold himself into the service of a slave trader in Africa and nearly died from sickness and starvation at the hands of his master's cruel wife. After being taken on board ship by a captain who had instructions from John's father to find and retrieve him, a great storm at sea threatened to destroy the vessel and drown the entire crew. But God had other plans. In the midst of the violent tempest, John Newton fell to his knees in desperation and cried out to God to have mercy upon his soul. There on that rickety, half-submerged ship, God answered his prayer and forgave him for his wicked ways. More than that, God transformed him into a brand new man, replacing his pursuit of sin with a love for Christ, holiness, and truth.

John went on to become a well-known and beloved minister of the gospel until the day of his death. Yet he never lost his sense of amazement that God would show such wondrous grace to a sinner such as himself. Near the end of John's life, some well-meaning friends suggested that he stop preaching. "I cannot stop," John nearly bellowed in reply. "What! Shall the old African blasphemer stop while he can speak?"[2] Before John passed into glory about two years later, he wrote an epitaph to be written on a plain marble tablet to mark his grave:

<blockquote>
John Newton, Clerk
Once an Infidel and Libertine,
A Servant of Slaves in Africa,
Was, by the rich mercy of our Lord and Savior
JESUS CHRIST
Preserved, restored, pardoned,
And appointed to preach the Faith
He had long laboured to destroy[3]
</blockquote>

Assuredly, John Newton was overwhelmed by the riches of God's grace. He preached, wrote, and sang of amazing grace from the day God saved him on that stormy sea, until the day the red damp earth was placed on his coffin fifty-nine years later.

My Discovery Of Sovereign Grace

During the summer of 1991, God began to overwhelm me with the same understanding of His grace that overwhelmed John Newton nearly two and a half centuries earlier. As pastor of a Bible church in Milpitas, California, I found myself teaching through the book of Romans in a verse-by-verse expository fashion. In Romans chapters eight and nine, I encountered some of the most hard-hitting teaching on sovereign grace in the Bible. I had made a commitment, however, to teach what I believed was the true meaning of the text, not what I wanted the text to mean. As I plowed through this section of God's Word with my congregation, God began to show me just how breathtaking His grace actually is.

At first I did not treasure the truths I discovered. In fact, at times I fought fiercely against them. Nevertheless, I earnestly desired to understand God's Word. I wanted to know the answer to such questions as, "Why are some people saved and others lost?" and "How exactly does a person come to Christ?" I had always thought I understood the answer to those questions. I believed the reason some were saved was simply because they made a decision to come to Christ. Furthermore, I had always assumed that a person came to Christ simply by exercising his free will to believe on Him. My study in the Scriptures, however, forced me to rethink those beliefs. It was extremely humbling and a bit frightening when I began to discover that I was not really the master of my fate or the captain of my destiny. It was hard to relinquish the idea that I was the one calling the shots. Furthermore, it was not easy to agree with God that in my unsaved condition I was spiritually dead, helpless to make a move toward Him. Yet, my understanding of the Bible led inescapably to these conclusions.

The truth of God's absolute sovereignty, especially in the arena of man's salvation, held a vise-like grip on my mind for months on end. For a solid year I could think of little else. I woke up thinking about God's sovereign grace and drifted off to sleep with this thought running through my mind. During the day I studied it in the Scriptures and meditated on my discoveries. During the ensuing year, I spent hundreds of hours reading books and listening to tapes dealing with this theme.

Interestingly, an amazing metamorphosis took place. The very truths which I yielded to only grudgingly because I could no longer deny them, slowly began to fill my heart with pleasure and delight. I found that my own experience echoed that of Charles Haddon Spurgeon's who wrote:

> When I was coming to Christ, I thought I was doing it all myself, and though I sought the Lord earnestly, I had no idea the Lord was seeking me. I do not think the young convert is at first aware of this. I can recall the very day and hour when

first I received those truths in my own soul - when they were, as John Bunyan says, burnt into my heart as with a hot iron, and I can recollect how I felt that I had grown on a sudden from a babe into a man - that I had made progress in Scriptural knowledge, through having found, once for all, the clue to the truth of God.[4]

With John Bunyan and Charles Spurgeon, I too felt God's red-hot iron as He burned the truths of sovereign grace into my soul. Jonathan Edwards, the great American theologian and philosopher of the 18th century, likewise stated:

From my childhood up, my mind had been full of objections against the doctrine of God's sovereignty in choosing whom He would to eternal life. . . It used to appear like a horrible doctrine to me. But I have often, since that first conviction, had quite another kind of sense of God's sovereignty than I had then. I have often since had not only a conviction, but a delightful conviction. The doctrine has very often appeared exceeding pleasant, bright and sweet. Absolute sovereignty is what I love to ascribe to God. But my first conviction was not so.[5]

Like Jonathan Edwards, the more time I spent considering the Biblical teaching of sovereign grace, the more delight I found in it.

My newfound Biblical discoveries caused me to grow in my understanding of God. The best way I can describe it is that my God suddenly grew much bigger. Contemplating His absolute power, majesty, and rule took my breath away. I no longer saw Him as grieving over those who would not let Him save them. Now I saw Him seated on His throne, working all things according to the counsel of His will.

My understanding of man also began to change. Whereas, before I thought of man as occupying the driver's seat, controlling his destiny through the use of his free will, I now understood that his sinful nature had enslaved his will so that he would choose only to reject God. I went from having a little God and a big man, to having a big God and a little man.

Additionally, I had to make some serious adjustments in my understanding of my role in evangelism. Up to this point, I fancied that getting someone converted was a relatively simple matter — all I had to do was put the right arguments and Scripture texts together persuasively enough. I now understood that man's condition is so sinful that only a miracle of grace will ever convert him. Furthermore, I began to look not just for a decision, raised hand, or sinner's prayer, but for evidence of God's work of grace upon a man's heart. My job, I now saw, was simply to present the gospel as purely and faithfully as I could; it was God's job to actually convert the sinner.

I also experienced a dramatic change in my attitude toward my salvation. In years past, I had thought that though God had saved me by His grace, I had to keep myself saved by my obedience and good works. I figured that my making it to heaven depended a great deal on me. I worried that if I did not keep up a rigorous lifestyle of prayer, Bible reading, church attendance, and good works, I might lose my salvation and end up in hell. Although it is true that we must persevere in faith in order to be saved (Hebrews 3:6,14; Colossians 1:21-23), I now understood that if I persevered in faith it was the result of God's eternal election. I realized that it is not so much my grasp on Him but His grasp on me that ultimately matters. As a result, I now enjoy a strong confidence that He who began a good work in me will perfect it until the day of Christ Jesus (Philippians 1:6).

God has quite literally overwhelmed me with His grace. I have a new vision of God, myself, evangelism, my salvation, and much more. It has helped me to see how greatly God loves me and has enabled me to rest secure in His purposes. In short, it has transformed my life. I can truthfully say that it has had nearly as great an impact on my life as my conversion. It is my heartfelt desire that this book will enable you to understand and appreciate your salvation more than ever before.

A word of caution though; this process will involve struggle. An individual will have to re-examine his cherished beliefs in the light of God's Word. He may have to modify a part of his belief system. That can be very painful. However, I am convinced that he will never regret the time and energy he invests in working through these issues.

The Meaning Of Grace

When God directs His grace toward sinful men, it is His unearned and undeserved favor to hell-deserving rebels. It is His unsought and unbought goodness, His sovereign favor, His royal generosity. Grace is what all men need, what none deserve, and what God alone can give. Because God is utterly holy and men are radically sinful, God must respond to men with wrath. Furthermore, God's grace is the only thing that can avert His wrath. Though all men deserve wrath, God chooses to bestow saving grace on some. Unless an individual becomes a recipient of the grace of God during his earthly life, he must spend eternity in the lake of fire (Revelation 20:11-15). That is how crucial it is to experience the grace of God.

I have known people who have been Christians for many years, who after a while come to look upon their salvation in a kind of blasé and ho-hum fashion. They seek after teachers who will give them something new. They want to go on to bigger and better things. I am convinced, however, that nothing can excel God's grace. Perhaps these believers do not need something new as much as they need to see more clearly something old. Perhaps they need to go back and restudy the most basic but wonderful truth of all - the sovereign grace of God.

I am convinced that when an individual understands God's sovereign grace, he will prize God, Christ, and his salvation in a deeper way than ever before. When an individual comes to understand the wonder of God's grace, he will want to fall on his knees and give Him the worship and the glory that He so rightly deserves for the rest of eternity. Rightly understood and appreciated, God's sovereign grace will change a person's life forever. He will never be the same.

As we begin to explore the grace of God, I encourage you to imitate the example of the Bereans who "received the word with great eagerness, examining the Scriptures daily, to see whether these things were so" (Acts 17:11). Put everything you read to the test of the Word of God. Take the time to look up each passage of Scripture that is cited and read it in its context. Seek diligently to discern truth from error. All human works are flawed - only God's Word is without error. Endeavor to adjust your understanding of God's grace as close to what the Bible teaches as you possibly can. As you do so, I trust you will be overwhelmed by grace!

NOTES:

1. John Newton, *The Works of John Newton,* Volume 3, (Carlisle, Pennsylvania: The Banner Of Truth Trust, 1985) 353.

2. John Newton, *The Works, Vol. 1,* 88.

3. John Newton, *The Works, Vol. 1,* 90.

4. C.H. Spurgeon, *C. H. Spurgeon Autobiography – Volume 1: The Early Years 1834-1859,* (Carlisle, Pennsylvania: The Banner of Truth Trust, 1962) 164-165.

5. Iain Murray, *Jonathan Edwards – A New Biography*, (Carlisle, Pennsylvania: The Banner of Truth Trust, 1987) 103.

Chapter 2

Our Desperate Need For Sovereign Grace

W hen God began to overwhelm me with His grace, one of the first things He did was help me to understand the Biblical teaching on the condition of unsaved men. The only way we can rightly appreciate God's grace is to realize how desperately we needed it. Ephesians 2:1-3 furnishes us with a thorough and graphic description of mankind in a state of sin:

> *And you were dead in your trespasses and sins, in which you formerly walked according to the course of this world, according to the prince of the power of the air, of the spirit that is now working in the sons of disobedience. Among them we too all formerly lived in the lusts of our flesh, indulging the desires of*

*the flesh and of the mind, and were by nature
children of wrath, even as the rest.*

If you were to come over to my house and go
into the family room, you would see several family
portraits hanging on the wall. We have had our family
picture taken almost every year since our eldest son
was born, and my wife has arranged the pictures very
nicely on the wall. However, there is one portrait in
particular that I am not fond of. For some reason,
the year this picture was taken I combed my hair
straight back so that it stands up tall and puffed out. I
don't know what possessed me. It is a horrible photo!
What's more, it is embarrassing. Some night when
everybody else is sleeping, I would like to sneak into
the family room, take down the picture, and burn it!

In the same way, the Apostle Paul in Ephesians
chapter two is showing us an old portrait of ourselves
that we would just as soon forget. It is our spiritual
portrait taken before we became Christians. It is a
ghastly and embarrassing sight. A friend of mine
carries around in his Bible an old picture of himself
which was taken a couple of weeks before he was
saved. He is wearing long, scraggly hair, donning
a T-shirt advertising an acid rock band, and looks
like he is high on drugs. He carries this old photo-
graph around with him so that he will never forget
the hellish life that God saved him from. Likewise,
in Ephesians 2 the apostle Paul is showing us the
hellish life that God saved us from.

We Were Dead In Our Sins

Ephesians 2:1 says, "And you were dead in your trespasses and sins." What does that mean? It can't possibly mean that we were dead *to* trespasses and sins. No, we were very much alive to them. Our text tells us that we formerly walked in them. It also cannot mean that we were dead to the world, because verse two tells us that we walked according to the course of this world. Furthermore, it cannot mean that we were dead to the flesh, because verse three tells us that we formerly lived in the lusts of the flesh, indulging the desires of the flesh and of the mind. Finally, it cannot mean that we were dead to the devil, because verse two tells us that we walked according to the prince of the power of the air, of the spirit that is now working in the sons of disobedience. When the apostle Paul says that we were dead in trespasses and sins, he does not mean that we were dead on those levels. No, the sad truth is that we were vibrantly alive to our sins, the world, the flesh, and the devil. We were biologically, socially, intellectually, and perhaps even morally alive; but we were spiritually dead. We were alive in every way except for one; we were dead to God. We were completely cut off from the life of God.

What does it mean to be dead in sins? A dead man has absolutely no power. He is helpless to do anything. If you were to go down to a mortuary, you could yell at a corpse for hours, but the man could never hear you. You could command him to open his eyes, speak to you, or stand up. You could do this hour after hour, but you would never elicit a response from him. He cannot even flicker his eyelashes. He cannot respond because he lacks the one thing needful - life. You can kick him or put a gun to his head and command that he speak to you, but the response will always be the same - nothing. He cannot see you, hear you, understand you, receive you, please you, or come to you. That is exactly the same situation we were in before God saved us.

The Man Dead In Sins Cannot See[1]

Jesus told Nicodemus in John 3:3, "Truly, truly, I say to you, unless one is born again, he cannot see the kingdom of God." Jesus goes on in verse five to tell Nicodemus that unless one is born again he cannot enter the kingdom of God. Thus, all who have been born again have entered God's kingdom and, having entered, are able to see it. If someone lived all their life in Europe, they would never be able to see the United States. In order to view the United States, an individual must first enter it. Likewise, in order for an individual to see the kingdom of God, he must first enter it. But entering the kingdom takes place only when God regenerates an individual. Thus, the unregenerate man cannot perceive the kingdom, for he is wholly outside of it.

But what is meant by seeing the "kingdom of God?" It cannot refer to heaven, for a man enters the kingdom when he is born again, not when he dies. It must refer, then, to that spiritual kingdom in which God rules and reigns by His Spirit in the lives of His people. In Romans 14:17 Paul identifies the characteristics of the kingdom as righteousness, peace, and joy in the Holy Spirit. Seen in this light, Jesus was instructing Nicodemus that unless a person is born again he can never see, understand, or experience the things of the Spirit which are discerned and enjoyed by the regenerate here upon the earth when they enter God's kingdom. Paul expressed this same truth in 1 Corinthians 2:14 in this manner, "But a natural [unsaved] man does not accept the things of the Spirit of God, for they are foolishness to him; and he cannot understand them, because they are spiritually appraised."

The Man Dead In Sins Cannot Hear

Jesus, in speaking to the religious leaders of His day, declared in John 8:43, "Why do you not understand what I am saying? It is because you cannot hear My word." Now, these religious leaders could hear the audible sounds that Jesus uttered. But they could not hear them with the internal ears of their heart. They could not embrace and receive Christ's word for they had no heart for it. Radio signals are all around us right now. If we were "tuned in," we might hear rock, jazz, classical, or country music. But we could never hear any of it without a stereo receiver. In the same way, a man remains stone deaf to the voice of Jesus Christ until he is born again. He lacks the "receiver" necessary to hear His voice. That "receiver" is a brand new heart that God gives to all those He causes to be born again.

The Man Dead In Sins Cannot Receive

Jesus told His disciples in John 14:16, "And I will ask the Father, and He will give you another Helper, that He may be with you forever; that is the Spirit of truth, whom the world cannot receive, because it does not behold Him or know Him, but you know Him because He abides with you, and will be in you." Just as a dead man cannot embrace you, so too a lost man cannot receive the Holy Spirit. He is spiritually helpless to do so, for he is not aware of Him and does not know Him.

The Man Dead In Sins Cannot Please

Paul tells us in Romans 8:7, "the mind set on the flesh [the mind of the unregenerate man] is hostile toward God; for it does not subject itself to the law of God, for it is not even able to do so; and those who are in the flesh cannot please God." We know that without faith it is impossible to please God (Hebrews 11:6). Before we became Christians we were without faith, and thus, spiritually powerless to please God.

The Man Dead In Sins Cannot Come

Jesus told us as much in John 6:44, "No one can come to Me, unless the Father who sent Me draws him." He said again in John 6:65, "For this reason I have said to you, that no one can come to Me, unless it has been granted him from the Father." Until the Father draws a man, he cannot come to Jesus Christ, being spiritually unable to make a move towards Him.

In spite of this clear teaching from God's Word, there are a number of different opinions today about the lost man's condition. For example, some believe that man is spiritually well. A British monk by the name of Pelagius in the early fifth century espoused this view, openly debating the teachings of Augustine on this issue. Pelagius taught that all men have the absolute equal ability at every moment to do good or evil. He believed that a man could live sinlessly. In his view, it is absolutely essential that we are able to keep all of God's commands, for if we cannot, then God was unfair in giving them to us. His slogan was, "Whatever I ought to do, I can do." Furthermore, Pelagius believed and taught that Adam's fall hurt only himself. Thus, according to his understanding, children are born neutral into the world, without a sinful nature.[2] This same basic view has been embraced today by some theological liberals who believe that all men are basically good. Given the proper environment and education, they say, men will live righteous lives.

There are others who believe that the unsaved man is spiritually sick. These individuals do not agree with Pelagius that man is spiritually well, because they realize that much of what he taught is contradictory to the Word of God. However, they do not believe that the unsaved person is as helpless as Augustine taught. Therefore, they have reached what is, for them, a happy medium. They believe that Adam's fall did deal a radical blow to the human race, but it did not leave him in a condition of total spiritual helplessness. In this system of thought, God graciously enables every sinner to repent and believe, but He does so in such a manner as not to interfere with man's freedom. According to them, every sinner possesses a free will and his eternal destiny depends on how he uses it. These individuals believe that man has the power to cooperate with God in obtaining salvation. They understand the condition of the sinner to be like a man who is drowning in a river. God throws the life rope to him. All he must do is reach out and hold onto the rope and let God pull him in to safety. Nevertheless, the decision to grasp the rope or let it slip through his fingers lies with him alone; God will not interfere with his decision.

Finally, there are others, myself included, who believe that man is not spiritually healthy or spiritually sick, but rather, spiritually dead. They believe that man cannot cooperate with God in obtaining salvation, because every part of man's being was affected by the fall, including his will. Thus, man is powerless to save himself or even cooperate with God in his own salvation. This was the position of Augustine as well as the reformers like Martin Luther and John Calvin. Salvation in this scheme is not determined by whether or not a man will choose of his free will to grasp the life rope that God throws to him. The reason is obvious; man is not just in trouble, needing a life rope tossed to him. He is dead at the bottom of the river. He needs God to dive down, bring him to shore, and then breathe His very life into him. Now, this may be very humbling to our natural pride, but it seems to me to be exactly what the apostle Paul is teaching here in Ephesians chapter two.

We Were Controlled By The World

Ephesians 2:2 tells us that we formerly walked "according to the course of this world." In referring to the "world," Paul is not speaking here of planet earth or all the people in the world. Rather, he is referring to the world of men alienated from God. He is declaring that formerly we ordered our behavior according to the course or path that the ungodly of this world walk in. We adopted their opinions, values, and attitudes. The world squeezed us into its mold. The phrase "according to" is from the Greek preposition "kata." Its root meaning is "down." It came to have the meaning of "to be dominated by."[3] Formerly, we were dominated by this evil world system. We were brainwashed by its propaganda. We had imbibed its philosophy of living for self and pleasure. Taking our cue from the world, we believed we could solve our problems. Thus, we did not need God and would not seek Him. Before God saved us we were unknowingly ruled by this present evil world.

We Were Controlled By The Devil

Additionally, Ephesians 2:2 tells us that we formerly walked "according to the prince of the power of the air, of the spirit that is now working in the sons of disobedience." The word "prince" comes from the Greek word which means "ruler." Jesus referred to the devil as the ruler of this world (John 12:13; 14:30; 16:11), and the Pharisees called him the ruler of the demons (Matthew 12:24). Paul referred to him as the "god" of this world (2 Corinthians 4:4). The devil is a ruler.

Who does he rule over? Our text says that he is the prince "of the power of the air." In Ephesians 6:12, Paul writes, "For our struggle is not against flesh and blood, but against the *rulers,* against the *powers*, against the world forces of this darkness, against the spiritual forces of wickedness in the heavenly places." In Ephesians 2:2 we again find the words "prince" (ruler) and "power." Therefore, since "rulers" and "powers" refer to evil spirits in Ephesians chapter six, it is extremely likely that they also refer to evil spirits in Ephesians 2:2. Thus, when we are told that Satan is the prince of the power of the air, it must mean that he is the ruler of all demon spirits. He rules over the kingdom of darkness. In other words, Satan is the five-star general commanding his army of hellish hosts.

Furthermore, we are told that "we formerly walked according to the spirit that is now working in the sons of disobedience." This does not mean that all lost men are indwelt by demons, but it does mean that they are subject to demonic influence. Unsaved men respond naturally to Satan's leading. Again the Greek preposition "kata" is used, meaning we were dominated not only by the world, but also by Satan and his wicked hosts. Imperceptibly to us, he was ruling over us, influencing us, tempting us, and holding us captive to do his will. We were absolutely controlled by him. This sobering truth is echoed elsewhere as well. Paul in writing to Timothy says, "the Lord's bond-servant must not be quarrel-some, but be kind to all, able to teach, patient when wronged, with gentleness correcting those who are in opposition, if perhaps God may grant them repentance leading to the knowledge of the truth, and they may come to their senses, and escape from the snare of the devil, *having been held captive by him to do his will*" (2 Timothy 2:24-26). Again the Apostle John wrote, "We know that we are of God, and *the whole world lies in the power of the evil one*" (1 John 5:19).

We Were Controlled By Our Flesh

What's more, we were also controlled by our flesh. Ephesians 2:2 informs us that we formerly walked in trespasses and sins. Just as a fish swims in water and a bird flies in the air, so we walked in sins. They were the natural element in which we lived. Everything we did in the sight of God was sin. Our deeds may have looked good to other people, but they were sinful in the sight of God, because they were not done out of faith in God, love to God, or for the glory of God. To illustrate, imagine that a doctor signs on with the United States Navy. While on board ship, he decides to mutiny and lead a crew of men in seizing the vessel. Eventually, a United States destroyer comes after them and a great gun battle ensues. When men on the doctor's ship are wounded, the doctor goes three days and nights without sleep in order to treat their injuries. Finally, the ship is captured. What will the United States government do to that man who gave so unstintingly of his time and energy? Will they give him a medal of honor for his sacrifice? Of course not. They will hang him! Why? Because all the good he did, was done in rebellion. His very goodness was evil.[4] So too, all our human goodness is evil in the sight of God, because it is all done in rebellion to Him. Until we surrender our lives to Christ in repentance and faith, "every intent of the thoughts of our heart is only evil continually" (Genesis 6:5).

Not only did we walk according to our sins, but Ephesians 2:3 tells us that we lived in the lusts of our flesh. Flesh, here, refers to man's fallen corrupt nature. We gave ourselves over to the lusts of our fallen nature. The lusts of our flesh were expressed in two different ways. Externally, our fleshly lusts expressed themselves in "indulging the desires of the flesh." We indulged in alcohol, drugs, sex, and anything else that arose from our bodily appetites. Internally, our fleshly lusts expressed themselves in "the desires of the mind" such as pride, envy, unbelief, strife, and selfishness. We "lived" in them. We gave ourselves over to fulfilling them. We were concerned with gratifying our fleshly desires in ways both external and internal. These lusts dominated and controlled us.

We Were Under The Wrath Of God

In Ephesians 2:3 Paul declares, "and were by nature children of wrath, even as the rest." When he says we were children of wrath "by nature," he means by physical birth. If that is true, then the ideas that babies are born into the world innocent and that children are under an "age of accountability" are myths. The Bible declares that they are born under the wrath of God and apart from a miracle of regeneration will be lost forever. This text in Ephesians is not the only passage that teaches this truth. We are taught elsewhere that we sinned in Adam (Romans 5:12), were brought forth in iniquity (Psalm 51:5), and are estranged from the womb (Psalm 58:3). All men are born under condemnation with three strikes against them. They are born DOA — dead on arrival!

Our text tells us that we were "children of wrath, even as the rest." We were no different than the rest of the world. In fact, we were in exactly the same condition as they are. Thus, if we are Christians and others are not, the reason does not lie in the fact that we are innately any better than they.

The sobering truth of this passage is that all men are born objects of the wrath of God. God's wrath is His holy response to sin. All sin is offensive and loathsome to His awesome purity and holiness. As long as we remain the sons of disobedience we must remain children of wrath. The only way, therefore, to escape the wrath of God is to cease being a son of disobedience. A son of disobedience is a person whose life is characterized by disobedience; a sinner

31

by nature. The only way, therefore, for a man to cease living as a son of disobedience is for God to change his nature so that he becomes a child of light producing the fruit of goodness, righteousness, and truth (Ephesians 5:8-9).

Conclusion

I trust that we can see more clearly now the sinner's desperate need for God's sovereign grace. We have seen from the Scriptures that if we are Christians, a miracle has taken place! We were dead in our sins, controlled by the world, the devil, and our flesh, and under the wrath of God. "We were once foolish, disobedient, deceived, enslaved to various lusts and pleasures, spending our life in malice and envy, hateful, hating one another" (Titus 3:3). We were in the snare of the devil, having been held captive by him to do his will (2 Timothy 2:26). Furthermore, "while we were still *helpless,* at the right time Christ died for the ungodly" (Romans 5:6). Do these texts seem to agree with the popular teaching that God wants to save everyone, but must wait until someone of his own free will lets Him? The texts describe us as dead, enslaved, captive, controlled, blind, deaf, helpless, hopeless, and powerless.

The popular understanding of free will is that all men possess the ability to repent of their sin and believe savingly on the Lord Jesus Christ at any time. However, if I am a slave, am I free? If I am held captive, do I have the freedom to leave? If I am blind, am I free to see? If I am deaf, am I free to hear? If I am dead, am I free to live? Of course not! Clearly then, the popular notion that the sinner's "free will" enables him to come to Christ in saving faith at any time, is at odds with the clear testimony of Scripture.

Rather, free will points to the liberty God has given man to make his own choices. When I go into a restaurant, I have the freedom to order anything on the menu (assuming I have the money to pay for it!). However, I will never voluntarily choose to spend my hard-earned money on cooked spinach. I detest spinach. My inclinations rise up against the very thought of ordering spinach in a restaurant. Likewise, the unsaved man will never choose to repent of his sins and commit his life to Christ on his own. God invites him to repent and trust Christ. More than that, God commands him to repent and trust in Christ. Nevertheless, the sinner will never accept God's invitation or obey His command to repent and believe for the simple reason that He does not want to. He will always choose sin over Christ. His mind is blinded (2 Corinthians 4:4); thus he thinks wrong thoughts about God. His heart is hard (Ephesians 4:18); thus he feels wrong emotions toward God. His will is corrupt (John 5:40); thus he chooses wrong actions in relation to God. His mind, emotions, and will are all in rebellion to God. Thus, he will never make the right choice in relationship to God unless God, of His own free grace, sovereignly grants him a new nature. Therefore, if we are Christians today, it had nothing to do with us and everything to do with our gracious heavenly Father. "Not to us, O Lord, not to us, but to Thy name give glory!" (Psalm 115:1).

The dark backdrop of man's sin and inability provides a wondrous setting to display the glory of God's grace. When you once understand and embrace the Biblical description of man as lost, helpless, and hopeless in his sin, you are now ready to glory in the magnificence of God's sovereign grace.

NOTES:

1. I am indebted to John Reisinger for his teaching at a men's retreat on March 3-5, 1995 in which he outlined what the unregenerate man cannot do.

2. Philip Schaff, *History of the Christian Church* (Peabody, Massachusetts: Hendrickson Publishers, Inc., 1996) 3:802-812.

3. Kenneth Wuest, *Word Studies in the Greek New Testament, Volume 1, Ephesians* (Grand Rapids, Michigan: Wm. B. Eerdmans Publishing Company, 1973) 61.

4. This illustration was taken from a tape by John Reisinger in which he was expounding the doctrine of total depravity.

Chapter 3

Electing Grace

W e have seen that the lost man's condition is
so desperate that he cannot save himself or
even cooperate with God in his salvation. His case,
humanly speaking, is hopeless. If he is ever to be
saved, God Himself must decide to reach out and
save Him by His own grace and power. The decree
of election is the truth that God has sovereignly
purposed to reach out and save a vast number of lost
and perishing souls, and that He has decided to do this
from eternity past without reference to man's works
or choice. A decree is simply an official royal decision. God is the King of the universe who has made
an official royal decision to save a definite number of
the human family.

I have found from personal experience that
whenever a person speaks or writes on sovereign
election, he is sure to get a response! He will find
that his hearers or readers are either passionately in

love with this truth, or recoil from it in horror. To some people, God's sovereign election is the most wonderful thing that they have ever discovered from the Scriptures. When they come to understand it, it is like getting saved all over again. To others, it is a devilish doctrine straight out of the pit of hell. I am sure that as I write upon this theme, there will be many different responses. I know that I am taking a risk by bringing up this subject at all, but I do so that it may enable you to gain a greater appreciation for your salvation than ever before. My only request is that you carefully and objectively weigh what the Scriptures teach on this subject. Remember, we must never base our beliefs on human opinion or speculation, but on the clear teaching of the Word of God. If an individual will read his Bible with an open and honest heart to see what it actually says about this subject, I believe God's truth will overwhelm him.

One thing is certain - an individual cannot avoid the subject of election if he accepts the Bible as the Word of God. The word "chosen" or some derivative thereof is found some thirty-six times in the New Testament. The word "elect" is found eight times. The word "predestined" is found seven times. In all, these words occur over fifty times in the New Testament alone. The truths of election and predestination are found in nearly every book of the New Testament. The doctrine of election simply cannot be avoided. A Christian must deal with it in one way or another. In order to do that, let us turn our attention to one of the premier texts on election in the New Testament — Ephesians 1:3-6:

Blessed be the God and Father of our Lord Jesus Christ, who has blessed us with every spiritual blessing in the heavenly places in Christ, just as He chose us in Him before the foundation of the world, that we should be holy and blameless before Him. In love He predestined us to adoption as sons through Jesus Christ to Himself, according to the kind intention of His will, to the praise of the glory of His grace, which He freely bestowed on us in the Beloved.

The phrase "He chose" is from the Greek verb "eklegomai" which means "to choose or pick out of."[1] The word "chosen" implies that not all are included. If I choose a banana out of a fruit basket, the rest of the fruit remains behind in the basket by default. Likewise, when God chose His people, some were selected while the rest were passed by. Furthermore, this Greek verb is in the middle voice[2] which means that God did it for Himself. God chose out of the mass of mankind a people for Himself to display His own glory.

The Preeminence Of Election

In Ephesians 1:3 Paul launches into a 202 word sentence in the Greek of praise to God. He tells us that God is to be blessed because He has blessed us with every spiritual blessing in the heavenly places in Christ. What are these blessings? The very first one that is mentioned is the blessing of election. Before mentioning our adoption, redemption, forgiveness, inheritance, or sealing, Paul mentions election. Election is mentioned first for the simple reason that every other blessing is dependent on it. If God has not appointed an individual to eternal life, that person will never receive any of these other blessings. Election is the foundation of every other blessing of God. All of the spiritual blessings God freely grants us have their source in His electing love. The whole process of salvation is the unfolding of God's electing love and predestined purpose. Election depends on God alone; all other blessings depend upon election.

The Author Of Election

Our text informs us, "*He* chose us." Who is the *He* mentioned here? Verse three answers our question by telling us that it was the God and Father of our Lord Jesus Christ. The author of election is God the Father. The Bible does not attribute our election to Jesus Christ or the Holy Spirit. The Father fulfills that role. Peter records the same in 1 Peter 1:1-2 by saying that his readers were "chosen by the foreknowledge of God the Father." Paul, in 1 Thessalonians 1:4 states, "knowing, brethren beloved by God, His choice of you." Each member of the blessed trinity has a role to play in God's eternal plan of salvation. The Father is the architect, the Son purchases the materials, and the Spirit builds the house. The Father chose those who would be saved,

Jesus Christ purchased their salvation, and the Holy Spirit infallibly applies the purchased salvation to their lives. If we are God's elect, we have God the Father to thank and bless for it.

The Objects Of Election

Our text says, "He chose *us*." Who is Paul talking about? Perhaps it would be helpful to note three different kinds of election found in Scripture: national, vocational, and salvational. National election is seen in God selecting the nation of Israel to fulfill His purposes (Deuteronomy 7:6-8). Vocational election is seen in God selecting different persons such as Abraham, Moses, Aaron, Peter, or Paul to fulfill a particular role such as leader, high priest, or apostle (Acts 9:15). The third type of election found in Scripture is salvational. This is what God does when He chooses individual persons to receive the gift of eternal life. Our text in Ephesians cannot be referring to national election, because Paul was not writing to a specific nation. He was writing to particular individual saints at Ephesus. He also could not have been referring to vocational election, because the people he wrote to were not chosen to be apostles, pastors, or other leaders. They were simple, ordinary believers predestined, not to a ministry role, but to adoption as sons (Ephesians 1:5). The objects of election in this text, therefore, are not a nation, nor a people called to a specific task, but rather God's people scattered throughout Asia Minor whom He chose to eternal life.

The Sphere Of Election

Our text clearly states, "He chose us *in Him*." This phrase teaches us that the decree of the Father does not take place apart from the person and work of Christ. It is accomplished only in Him and by virtue of His work. The finished work of Christ is the means by which election becomes effectual in human history. Election alone saves no one. It determines the *who*, but not the *how* of salvation. The cross of Christ carries out the Father's eternal plan. That is why, after describing the Father's role in election in Ephesians 1:4-6, the apostle Paul goes on to describe Christ and His work in carrying out the Father's plan in Ephesians 1:7-12.

The phrase "in Him" also teaches us that God chose us by uniting us to His Son before the foundation of the world. In other words, before time began, the Father chose Jesus Christ to be the Redeemer of His people (Isaiah 42:1), and gave these people to His Son to be the reward of His obedience and suffering (John 17:2,9,24; Isaiah 53:10-12). The elect were placed into Christ's hands from eternity (John 10:28-29). Christ came to be their representative - to be born, live, die, and rise again on their behalf. All that the Son did, He did for His people, because He represented them by a decree of His Father from all eternity.

The Timing Of Election

When were these individuals chosen to salvation? Again, we find the answer to this fascinating question in our text as it declares, "He chose us in Him *before the foundation of the world*." The mind-boggling truth is that before the universe existed, God Almighty had already laid out a plan which included the exact number and identity of every person He would ever save. Notice how the following texts define the timing of election:

Revelation 17:8: "And those who dwell on the earth will wonder, whose name has not been written in the book of life *from the foundation of the world*, when they see the beast, that he was and is not and will come." If some names were not written in the book of life from the foundation of the world, the obvious implication is that some names *were* written in the book of life from the foundation of the world. In contrast to much popular teaching then, it is not true that a person's name is inscribed in the book of life when they "accept Christ." On the contrary, their name was recorded before the foundation of the world was laid.

2 Timothy 1:9: "who saved us, and called us with a holy calling, not according to our works, but according to His own purpose and grace which was granted us in Christ Jesus *from all eternity*." God's purpose to save us arose from His own sovereign will, not when we believed on Christ, but from all eternity.

2 Thessalonians 2:13: "But we should always give thanks to God for you, brethren beloved by the Lord, because God has chosen you *from the beginning* for salvation through sanctification by the Spirit and faith in the truth." In this passage Paul again emphasizes that God did not choose to save us as a result of our choice of Him, but rather chose us from the beginning.

Matthew 25:34: "Then the King will say to those on His right, 'Come, you who are blessed of My Father, inherit the kingdom prepared for you *from the foundation of the world.*'"

These texts of Scripture show us that God does everything in time according to an eternal plan, or as the Scripture puts it, "He works all things after the counsel of His will" (Ephesians 1:11). From eternity past, the whole plan of redemption down to the most minute detail was designed of God. Thus, all is certain. There is no possibility of failure or of a change of plan.

Augustus Toplady, the 18th century author of the well-known hymn "Rock Of Ages", illustrated the timing of election in these words:

> The book of life, or decree of election, is the marriage-register of the saints in which their everlasting espousal to Christ stands indelibly

recorded by the pen of God's free and eternal love. . . The elect were betrothed to Christ from everlasting in the covenant of grace. They are actually married to Him and join hands with Him in conversion, but they are not taken home to the bridegroom's house until death dismisses them from the body.[3]

The famous Baptist preacher, Charles Spurgeon once quipped, "I am sure He chose me before I was born, or else He never would have chosen me afterward!"[4]

The Results Of Election

The results of God's eternal decree of election are two-fold.

The first result of God's eternal decree is that we should be holy and blameless before Him. This wonderful, two-sided blessing begins to take place at the moment of our justification. When a sinner believes on Jesus Christ, God clothes him in His righteous garments. It is as though he had never sinned, but is instead covered by the righteousness of Christ. Nevertheless, the believer will not demonstrate perfect righteousness until he stands glorified in Christ's presence. Then he shall be absolutely holy before Him in practice as well as position. Christ's blazing eyes of holiness will not be able to detect any sin in him at all. This is the truth of Ephesians 5:25-27: "Husbands, love your wives, just as Christ also loved the church and gave Himself up for her; that He might sanctify her, having cleansed her by the washing of water with the word, that He might present to Himself the church in all her glory, having no spot or wrinkle or any such thing; but that she should be holy and blameless." That is the culmination of God's work in us from the moment of our conversion — our absolute and complete conformity to the Lord Jesus Christ.

Also, note that holiness is a fruit of election, not the cause of it. He chose us that we should be holy, not because we already were. God does not choose us because we are holier than others. He chooses so that we will become holy and blameless before Him.

The second result of God's eternal decree is that we should be adopted as His sons. Adoption is the act of God whereby He brings men from Adam's ruined family into His own, making them His own children, and granting them all the rights and privileges of His own sons. All men are born into the family of Satan (John 8:44). No one has a right to be in God's family. However, God, of His own sheer mercy and grace, decided that He would not permit the whole world to perish in hell, but would adopt a multitude of sinners, conform them to the image of His Son, and bring them to eternal glory. This is the truth of Romans 8:29 where it states, "For whom He foreknew, He also predestined to become conformed to the image of His Son, that He might be the first-born among many brethren."

The Motive Of Election

Our text in Ephesians goes on to state, "*In love* He predestined us to adoption as sons through Jesus Christ to Himself." Here we are told the reason God chose us to be holy and blameless and to be His adopted children. It was because of His eternal, unchanging, and sovereign electing love. God loves all His creatures with a general love of benevolence, but He loves His elect with a special, discriminating, saving love. It is interesting to note how often in Scripture the love of God and His decree of election are coupled together.

Colossians 3:12: "And so, as those who have been *chosen* of God, holy and *beloved*, put on a heart of compassion, kindness, humility, gentleness and patience."

1 Thessalonians 1:4: "knowing, brethren *beloved* by God, His *choice* of you."

2 Thessalonians 2:13: "But we should always give thanks to God for you, brethren *beloved* by the Lord, because God has *chosen* you from the beginning for salvation through sanctification by the Spirit and faith in the truth."

Augustus Toplady in referring to this great theme of God's electing love wrote, "God's everlasting love, His decree of election, and eternal covenant of redemption are the three hinges on which the door of man's salvation turns."[5]

The Cause Of Election

Why did God choose some and pass by others? Ephesians 1:5 tells us that it was *"according to the kind intention of His will."* The Authorized version translates this "according to the good pleasure of His will." Seen in this light, God's choice was according to His good pleasure. At first glance this may seem as if God were arbitrary and capricious, taking delight in choosing some and damning others. However, we should never view election as if God were up in heaven rolling dice to see who gets chosen. He is not a celestial child crying gleefully, "eenie, meenie, miney, moe!" If we were chosen by God, it is not just because we got lucky. Luck had nothing to do with it. The kind intention of His will had everything to do with it. God had a reason for choosing whom He did. We do not know what that reason was, but we do know that it had nothing to do with our own personal worthiness. The reason is to be found in God alone, not in those He has chosen. Because God has not seen fit to fill us in on all the details of that purpose, we must simply trust Him in those things He has not fully revealed to us. "The secret things belong to the Lord our God, but the things revealed belong to us and to our sons forever" (Deuteronomy 29:29).

A person may fully intend to go to the dentist and also to plant a beautiful rose garden. Both are decisions of his will, but the latter alone is according to his good pleasure. Likewise, God's choice to save us was a matter of delight to Him. We get a hint of this in Luke 10:21 where Jesus rejoices greatly in the Holy Spirit and says, "I praise Thee O Father, Lord of heaven and earth, that Thou didst hide these things from the wise and intelligent and didst reveal them to babes. Yes, Father, for thus it was *well-pleasing* in Thy sight."

I find it extremely interesting that in the entire text of Ephesians 1:3-14, nothing is stated about the sinner's will. We are not told that God chose us according to our will. Divine election is not conditioned upon our faith, our repentance, or our good works. These things are the fruits of election, not the root. Paul, as emphatically as he possibly could, stated this truth in Romans 9:16, "So then it *does not* depend on the man who wills or the man who runs, but on God who has mercy."

The Goal Of Election

What was God's goal in this entire matter? According to Ephesians 1:6, it was all for "the praise of the glory of His grace." We see then, that God's glory is the goal behind all He does. This comes out quite clearly all the way through this paragraph. In verses 3-6 Paul describes the work of God the Father, and caps it off by saying it was "to the praise of the glory of His grace." In verses 7-12 Paul describes the work of Jesus Christ, and sums it up by saying it was "to the praise of His glory." In verses 13-14 Paul describes the work of the Holy Spirit, and says it was "to the praise of His glory." In this entire section of Scripture, the apostle Paul is calling on us to bless God for His glorious grace. The grace of God shines most resplendently when seen in the light of sovereign election. Oh, how glorious is His grace! From eternity past He has set His love upon us, knowing what rebels and sinners we would be. He chose to have mercy upon us, adopt us into His own family, give us all the rights of legitimate sons, grant us an inheritance, wipe out all our sins, and make us holy and blameless before Him forever. It is absolutely incredible! John Calvin, the 16th century reformer, put it this way: "He [Paul] extols sublimely the grace of God toward the Ephesians to rouse their hearts to gratitude, to set them all aflame, to occupy and fill them with this thought."[6]

Has the electing love of God roused our heart to gratitude, set us all aflame, and filled us with this thought? Are we ravished by the knowledge of His distinguishing grace towards us? I truly hope so.

Conclusion

Oh the glory of the grace of God! The Biblical teaching on divine election highlights God's sovereign grace like few other truths in His Word. A friend and fellow pastor[7] uses the following illustration to teach the exceeding sweetness of God's sovereign election. He asks the ladies in his congregation to imagine that they have just got married, and are driving away from the church parking lot to go on their honeymoon. The new husband turns to her and says, "Honey, I want to share something with you. The first time I ever laid eyes on you I decided that one day you'd be mine, because I loved you so much. Do you remember when you were just a child and had to have that expensive operation? Everyone thought you were going to die. Your parents didn't know where they were going to get the money, until one day they found a large check in the mail. Well, I'm the one that sent that check. You never knew where it came from, but it was me. As you were growing up, you kept getting cards in the mail that said "from your secret admirer." You never realized it, but that was me as well. I determined that I loved you so much that I would do whatever it took to win you." If a woman heard those words from her husband, would she stomp her feet and shout, "How dare you violate my free will?!" No, rather she would say, "That's the loveliest thing I've ever heard in all my life!" Likewise, the believer who understands that God set His love upon him from all eternity and did whatever was necessary to overcome his resistance and draw him to Christ, sees this truth as altogether glorious.

NOTES:

1.   Joseph Henry Thayer, *The New Thayer's Greek-English Lexicon*, Peabody, Massachusetts: Hendrickson Publishers, Inc., 1979) 196.

2. Barbara & Timothy Friberg, *Analytical Greek New Testament* (Grand Rapids, Michigan: Baker Book House, 1981) 588.

3. Augustus Toplady, *The Works of Augustus Toplady*, (Harrisonburg, Virginia: Sprinkle Publications, 1987) 544-545.)

4. John Blanchard, *Gathered Gold* (England: Evangelical Press, 1984) 78.

5. Toplady, 554.

6. John Calvin, *Calvin's Commentaries, The Epistles of Paul the Apostle to the Galatians, Ephesians, Philippians and Colossians* (Grand Rapids, Michigan: Wm. B. Eerdmans Publishing Company, 1965) 123.

7. This illustration is taken from a taped sermon by Mark Webb, pastor of Grace Bible Church in Olive Branch, Mississippi, entitled, *The Doctrine of Election.*

Chapter 4

Redeeming Grace: The Sufficiency of the Atonement

⸺

N ot only is it true that God's grace is desperately needed, it is equally true that it was sovereignly secured. Whereas grace was sovereignly decreed by God the Father in election, it was sovereignly secured by God the Son at the cross. There at Calvary, our incomparable Savior secured the eternal salvation of all God's chosen people.

When one surveys all the Biblical teaching concerning the atonement of Christ, he will find that some passages seem to indicate that Christ's work at the cross was sufficient for all men, whereas others point to a definite design in His death to save His elect. It is only as we seek to embrace all that the Scriptures teach about the death of Christ that we will see the full glory of Christ's work of redemption. This comprehensive view of Christ's atoning work can be summed up in the motto, "Christ died sufficiently for all, but effectively only for the elect." Often the atonement of Christ[1] is viewed with only one aspect in mind: either as strictly limited in its intention to save the elect alone, or offered equally for all men alike with no absolute intention to save a chosen people at all. I believe that both of these views of the atonement, though containing truth, fall short of embracing the whole counsel of God upon this vital subject.

Many believers view Christ's work on the cross as though a man walked into a hardware store and laid down just enough money to buy the tools that he wanted. Others view Christ's work as though the man laid down enough money to buy everything in the store, without any intention of taking any specific items home with him. A more accurate way to view the redemption of Christ is of a man who goes into a hardware store, lays down enough money to buy everything in the store as well as the building itself, and then takes out of it those items he wants. The atoning work of Christ, in and of itself, is sufficient to save every sinner who has ever or will ever live. However, it was only designed to save God's elect.

In order to grasp the greatness of what Christ accomplished at Calvary, we need to explore the sufficiency, design, and benefits of His atonement. In this chapter we will focus on the sufficiency of Christ's atoning work.

There are many passages of Scripture which reveal that Christ's death is sufficient to save all men.

The Biblical Testimony

Isaiah 53:6: "All of us like sheep have gone astray, each of us has turned to his own way; but the Lord has caused the iniquity of us *all* to fall on Him." Notice in this passage that the same *all* that have gone astray and turned to their own ways are the same *all* whose iniquity was laid on Christ. Thus, the extent of the sins laid on Christ must exactly parallel the extent of sin in the world, for the Scriptures dogmatically affirm that the entire human race has turned aside from the path of God's righteousness, and have fallen short of the glory of God (Romans 3:10-12, 23). Therefore, Christ, as our sin-bearing substitute, suffered sufficiently for all.

John 1:29: "Behold, the Lamb of God who takes away the sin of *the world*!" Here we are told that Christ, in the sacrifice of Himself as the Lamb of God, would take away the sin of the whole world. Although some expositors interpret the *world* as the elect scattered throughout the world, it must be admitted that there is nothing in this text itself that demands that we understand this term in such a restricted manner. Rather, it would appear that this conclusion is founded upon a previously defined system of theology brought to bear upon the passage. It is interesting that John Calvin, the influential reformer, did not deem it necessary to understand the *world* in this text in that narrow sense. In his commentary on this verse, John Calvin states:

when he says *the sin of the world* he extends this kindness indiscriminately to the whole human race, that the Jews might not think the Redeemer has been sent to them alone. From this we infer that the whole world is bound in the same condemnation; and that since all men without exception are guilty of unrighteousness before God, they have need of reconciliation. John, therefore, by speaking of the sin of the world in general, wanted to make us feel our own misery and exhort us to seek the remedy. Now it is for us to embrace the blessing offered to all, that each may make up his mind that there is nothing to hinder him from finding reconciliation in Christ if only, led by faith, he comes to Him.[2]

John 3:16: "For God so loved *the world*, that He gave His only begotten Son, that whoever believes in Him should not perish, but have eternal life." Although some Christians believe that *world* here refers to the world of the elect, the Greek lexicons are unanimous in defining it as humankind. Thus, it seems far better to take the expression as referring simply to the race of Adam. God so loved the human race that He did not permit all of mankind to perish in hell. Rather, He gave His only begotten Son to die for guilty sinners, in order that *whoever* believes in Him should not perish, but have eternal life.

If Jesus had meant to designate the elect by the expression "the world," He could have made His meaning much more clear by simply saying, "For God so loved the elect, that He gave His only begotten

Son, that the elect should not perish, but have eternal life." However, Jesus seems to imply a distinction between the world that God loved and gave Christ for, and "whoever believes" out of that world. Thus, "the world" must refer to the world of Adam's race whom God loved and gave Christ for. However, only those who believe in Christ from among this world of sinners will not perish, but have eternal life.

The apostle Paul writes to this effect in his letter to Titus, "But when the kindness of God our Savior and His love *for mankind* appeared, He saved us" (Titus 3:4). To be sure, the love of God mentioned in this text is not the same as that saving love of God directed towards His chosen people from all eternity taught in other passages of Scripture (Ephesians 1:4-6; Colossians 4:12; 2 Thessalonians 2:13). However, it surely includes a genuine compassion and pity towards sinners as sinners.

Furthermore, it must be remembered that John 3:16 follows on the heels of verses 14 and 15 in which Jesus refers to Moses lifting up the serpent in the wilderness, so that "any man" who was bitten could look to it and live (Numbers 21:9). Jesus teaches here that the bronze serpent lifted up was a type of Him being lifted upon the cross in order that "whoever" believes might have eternal life.

Indeed, Bishop John Charles Ryle, in his commentary on John 3:16 writes:

> it seems to me a violent straining of language
> to confine the word "world" to the elect. "The
> world" is undoubtedly a name sometimes given

to the "wicked" exclusively. But I cannot see that it is a name ever given to the saints. For another thing, to interpret the word "world" of the elect only is to ignore the distinction which, to my eyes, is plainly drawn in the text between the whole of mankind and those out of mankind who "believe." If the "world" means only the believing portion of mankind, it would have been quite enough to say, "God so loved the world, that he gave his only begotten Son, that the world should not perish." But our Lord does not say so. He says, "that whosoever believeth," *i.e.*, that whosoever out of the world believeth.[3]

Along the same lines, John Calvin has written of this verse of Scripture in his commentaries:

Christ brought life because the heavenly Father does not wish the human race that He loves to perish… He has used a general term [whosoever], both to invite indiscriminately all to share in life and to cut off every excuse from unbelievers. Such is also the significance of the term 'world' which He had used before. For although there is nothing in the world deserving of God's favour, He nevertheless shows He is favourable to the whole world when He calls all without exception to the faith of Christ, which is indeed an entry into life.[4]

John 3:16 then, indicates that God loved and gave His Son for the race of Adam, that anyone from that race who believes in Christ might be saved. Surely then, this passage teaches that there is a sufficiency in the death of Christ for all men without exception.

2 Corinthians 5:18-20: "Now all these things are from God, who reconciled us to Himself through Christ, and gave us the ministry of reconciliation, namely, that God was in Christ reconciling *the world* to Himself, not counting their trespasses against them, and He has committed to us the word of reconciliation. Therefore, we are ambassadors for Christ, as though God were entreating through us; we beg you on behalf of Christ, be reconciled to God." In verse 19 Paul states that God was in Christ reconciling the world to Himself. However, in verse 20 he exhorts his readers to be reconciled to God. How is it possible that God had already reconciled the world to Himself, and yet some people still needed to be reconciled to God? Apparently, Christ in His death achieved the possibility of reconciliation for all men, although actual reconciliation does not take place until the Holy Spirit effectually applies Christ's death to the sinner by uniting him to Christ.

1 Timothy 2:3-6: "This is good and acceptable in the sight of God our Savior, who desires *all men* to be saved and to come to the knowledge of the truth. For there is one God, and one mediator also between God and *men*, the man Christ Jesus, who gave Himself as a ransom *for all*, the testimony borne at the proper time." Paul expressly states not only that God desires *all men* to be saved, but that Christ as mediator gave Himself as a ransom for *all*. Although some commentators argue that the *all* in verses 4 and 6 mean no more than all *kinds* or all *without distinction*, again we must affirm that this interpretation is not required by the context, but instead seems to be deduced in order to harmonize with a previously held system of theology.

This passage, if taken in its natural and obvious sense, indicates that in some sense, Christ's death was offered for and made available to all men. Because God desires the salvation of all, He has sent His Son to make a sufficient atonement for all. Of course, this *desire* on the part of God for the salvation of all men is not the same thing as His sovereign *purpose* to save those He has chosen from eternity past. Yet, it does express His sincere and heartfelt desire for their salvation. In accordance with that desire, Christ has laid the groundwork for their reconciliation in His death, so that any man who avails himself by faith of Christ's atoning work, elect or not, will be saved.

1 Timothy 4:10: "For it is for this we labor and strive, because we have fixed our hope on the living God, who is the Savior of *all men*, especially of believers." Paul, in this text, points out that the living God is the Savior of all men in one sense, but especially the Savior of believers in another sense. The term "Savior" should be understood in the sense of one who reconciles us to God and redeems us from sin, as it is used earlier in this epistle (1 Timothy 2:3-6). Yet, how can it be said that God is both the Savior of all men, and also especially of those who believe?

The answer must lie in the dual work of Christ at the cross. There in His cross-work, Christ made a sufficient provision of salvation for all men. Hence, He can truly be called the Savior of all men. However, in addition to making a sufficient provision of salvation for all, He secured the actual salvation of all those who would ever believe, and thus is *especially* the Savior of the elect.

Titus 2:11: "For the grace of God has appeared, bringing salvation to *all men*." The salvation of sinners is based upon the person and work of Jesus Christ. Yet, this passage teaches us that it has been brought to all men. This surely must indicate that Christ in His death has made salvation available to and sufficient for all men.

Hebrews 2:9: "But we do see Him who has been made for a little while lower than the angels, namely, Jesus, because of the suffering of death crowned with glory and honor, that by the grace of God He might taste death for *everyone*." We are told very clearly that Christ tasted death for everyone in this passage. The Greek word for everyone (*pantos*) means "each or every." The emphasis in this passage is that Christ died sufficiently for each and every person. At the same time, the context indicates that He had a particular design in His death towards the many sons He would bring to glory, those who are sanctified, His brethren, and the children God had given Him (Hebrews 2:10-13). Although He tasted death for everyone, Christ died especially for the elect.

2 Peter 2:1: "But false prophets also arose among the people, just as there will also be false teachers among you, who will secretly introduce destructive heresies, even denying the Master *who bought them*, bringing swift destruction upon themselves." Peter in this text instructs his readers that false teachers would come among them who would deny the Master who bought them. The word for "bought" in Greek is *agaradzo*. It is the Greek word commonly used to buy or purchase something. Sometimes it refers to the redemption of Christ at the cross (1 Corinthians 6:20; Revelation 5:9; 14:3). That appears to be the meaning in this passage, as it is difficult to understand how the Master bought them in any other way. If that is the case, then these false teachers who will bring swift destruction upon themselves, were "bought" in some sense by Christ's redeeming work, even though they end up being destroyed. It would appear then, that a general provision was made for all men in Christ's death.

1 John 2:2: "and He Himself is the propitiation for our sins; and not for ours only, but also for those of *the whole world*." John in this passage is referring to Jesus Christ the righteous (1 John 2:1) and assures believers that Christ is their propitiation who averts God's wrath from them. However, at the same time, he informs them that Christ is also the propitiation for those of the whole world. In the very same epistle, John mentions the phrase *whole world* again saying, "the *whole world* lies in the power of the evil one" (1 John 5:19). Here *whole world* refers to all the unregenerate of the human race, for it is they who remain under the dominion of Satan. Thus, when John says that Christ is the propitiation not only for believers, but also for the sins of the whole world, he must mean that this propitiation is sufficient to save any man in the entire world. Of course, the majority of those throughout the world will never avail themselves of Christ's atoning death in order to be saved from God's wrath. However, John indicates in this passage that Christ as a propitiation for sin, is available to them, elect or not. Here we see the all-sufficiency of Christ's sacrificial death for the sins of all mankind.

Three Views of the Atonement

There are three primary views of the extent of Christ's atonement: universal, particular, and dualistic. The Universal View states that Christ died equally for all men. The Particular View states that Christ died for the elect alone. The Dualistic View asserts that Christ died for all, but especially for the elect. Perhaps these different ways of looking at Christ's work on the cross can best be understood by a simple illustration.

The Universal View of Christ's atonement can be illustrated by imagining that a ship with hundreds of passengers goes down at sea. Before the ship sinks, an officer wires for help. An hour later, a rescue ship arrives big enough to take in all the shipwrecked passengers. The captain of the rescue ship notices hundreds of bodies bobbing up and down in the ocean, clutching planks and debris in order to stay afloat. The captain calls out from his megaphone, "Anyone who would like to be rescued, raise your hand, and I will take you to safety!" Many hands go up all over the water, and the captain responds by hauling them into his ship and taking them safely to shore.

Now let's change the illustration a little to see the Particular View of Christ's atonement. Again we have a passenger ship that goes down at sea. But this time a man offshore finds out that his wife and four children were on the ship that has sunk. In order to save his family, he takes a six-passenger motorboat, and speeds out to the site where the ship went down. There, as he observes hundreds of people bobbing up and down in the water, he spies his own family. Passing by the drowning multitudes, he directs his small craft to his family, hauls them in, and takes them to safety, while the rest perish at sea.

There are serious difficulties with both the Universal and Particular views of the atonement. The Universal View is represented by a man with a ship big enough to save all, but its captain goes out to save no one in particular. There is no definite design in his rescue mission. However, the Scriptures clearly teach that Christ had a definite people in mind when He went to the cross. The Bible teaches that Christ gave His life a ransom for *many,* that He laid down His life for the *sheep,* that He loved the *church* and gave Himself up for *her* (Matthew 20:28; John 10:11; Ephesians 5:25). Christ did not die for a vague, nameless blob of humanity. Rather, He died to save all those the Father had given Him (John 17:2,9,19).

On the other hand, the Particular View sees Christ's mission as the man who went out to save his family in a boat only big enough to save his wife and children. This view fails to do justice with those many texts which ascribe an infinite and inexhaustible sufficiency to the cross of Christ. The Scripture declares that Christ was the lamb of God who took away the sins of the *world*, that He gave His life a ransom for *all*, that He tasted death for *everyone*, and that He is a propitiation not for believers only, but also for the sins of the *whole world* (John 1:29; 1 Timothy 2:6; Hebrews 2:9; 1 John 2:2).

Furthermore, those who hold to the Particular View, must agree that the man in the illustration is unable to give a sincere invitation for all those perishing in the sea to be saved, for even if they did desire to be saved, he has no room in his little boat for them. However, the Scriptures leave us in no doubt that God's invitations and offers of salvation to all men are sincere and genuine. "Turn to Me, and be saved, all the ends of the earth; for I am God, and there is no other" (Isaiah 45:22). "As I live!" declares the Lord God, "I take no pleasure in the death of the wicked, but rather that the wicked turn from his way and live. Turn back, turn back from your evil ways! Why then will you die, O house of Israel!" (Ezekiel 33:11). "And he sent out his slaves to call those who had been invited to the wedding feast, and they were unwilling to come" (Matthew 22:3).

Happily, there is another view which avoids these pitfalls, and allows one to accept all of the Scriptural instructions about Christ's sacrifice at face value. In order to understand this view (the Dualistic View), imagine that the United States is at war with Cuba. A man's family is taken captive as prisoners of war, and are being taken back to Cuba across the Gulf of Mexico in a Cuban warship, when a violent storm capsizes the ship and causes it to sink. A man in Texas receives word that the warship his family was traveling on has gone down at sea, and being a captain in the United States Navy himself, goes out to rescue them in a massive naval ship. When he arrives, he quickly locates his family, and hauls them into the ship. Having rescued his family, he then calls out into his megaphone to the hundreds of drowning enemies, "If you would like me to take you to safety, just raise your hand!" Because of their bitter hostility to their avowed enemies, these Cuban sailors would sooner die than be saved by the United States Navy, and so all alike refuse the invitation. After sincerely and urgently offering again and again to bring anyone who wishes to safety, the man finally turns around and sadly heads back to shore.

In this illustration, the ship captain had a definite people in mind in his mission. He went to save his family. At the same time, his boat was capable of saving all those drowning at sea, and his invitations and pleadings were sincere. Likewise, the Scriptures teach that Christ in His death, had a definite design to save His elect, while at the same time made a sufficient provision for all.

Voices From Our Evangelical Heritage

John Calvin, in Book III of his Institutes states:

How do we receive those benefits which the Father bestowed on his only-begotten Son – not for Christ's own private use, but that he might enrich poor and needy men? First, we must understand that as long as Christ remains outside of us, and we are separated from him, *all that he has suffered and done for the salvation of the human race* remains useless and of no value for us. Therefore, to share with us what he has received from the Father, he had to become ours and to dwell within us. . . for, as I have said, all that he possesses is nothing to us until we grow into one body with him.[5] [emphasis mine]

It's obvious from this statement that Calvin viewed Christ's sacrifice as offered on behalf of the human race, yet not actually saving any man until he is actually united to Christ.

Recognizing the sufficiency of the atonement of Christ, the framers of the Canons of the Synod of Dort wrote in 1619:

The death of the Son of God is the only and most perfect sacrifice and satisfaction for sin; is of infinite worth and value, abundantly sufficient to expiate the sins of the whole world. . . And, whereas many who are called by the gospel do not repent nor believe in Christ, but perish in unbelief;

this is not owing to any defect or insufficiency in the sacrifice offered by Christ upon the cross, but is wholly to be imputed to themselves.[6]

Likewise, Jonathan Edwards, one of the great thinkers of church history, in his sermons has stated:

Christ, having fully satisfied for all sin, or having wrought out a satisfaction that is sufficient for all, it is now no way inconsistent with the glory of the divine attributes to pardon the greatest sins of those who in a right manner come unto Him for it.[7]

John Newton, in reflecting upon the question of the extent of Christ's atonement wrote:

The extent of the atonement is frequently represented, as if a calculation had been made, how much suffering was necessary for the surety to endure, in order exactly to expiate the aggregate number of all the sins of all the elect; that so much He suffered precisely, and no more; and that when this requisition was completely answered, He said, "It is finished, bowed His head, and gave up the ghost." But this nicety of computation does not seem analogous to that unbounded magnificence and grandeur which overwhelm the attentive mind in the contemplation of the divine conduct in the natural world. When God waters the earth, He waters it abundantly. He does not restrain the rain to cultivated or improvable spots, but, with a profusion of bounty worthy of Himself, His clouds pour down water with equal abundance upon the barren mountain, the lonely desert, and the pathless ocean. Why may we not say, with the Scripture, that Christ died to "declare the righteousness of God," to manifest that He is just in justifying the ungodly who believe in Jesus? And for anything we know to the contrary, the very same display of the evil and demerit of sin, by the Redeemer's agonies and death, might have been equally necessary, though the number of the elect were much smaller than it will appear to be when they shall all meet before the throne of glory."[8]

Charles Hodge, Professor at Princeton Seminary for fifty-eight years writes:

As no limit can be placed on the dignity of the eternal Son of God who offered Himself for our sins, so no limit can be assigned to the meritorious value of His work. It is a gross misrepresentation of the Augustinian doctrine to say that it teaches that Christ suffered so much for so many, and that He would have suffered more had a greater number of people been included in the purpose of salvation. This is not the doctrine of any Church on earth and never has been. What was sufficient for one was sufficient for all. Nothing less than the light and heat of the sun is sufficient for any one plant or animal. But what is absolutely necessary for each is abundantly sufficient for the infinite number and variety of plants and animals which fill the earth. All that Christ did and suffered would have been necessary had only one human soul been the object of redemption, and nothing different and nothing more would have been required had every child of Adam been saved through His blood... Christ fulfilled the conditions of the covenant under which all men were placed. He rendered the obedience required of all and suffered the penalty which all had incurred; therefore, His work is equally suited to all. . . Augustinians readily admit, however, that the death of Christ had a relation to the whole human family as well. It is the ground on which salvation is offered to every creature under heaven who hears the gospel. . . In view of the effects which the death of Christ produces on the relation of all mankind to God, it has in all ages been customary with Augustinians to say that Christ died sufficiently for all, but efficaciously only for the elect. There is a sense, therefore, in which He died for all, and there is a sense in which He died for the elect alone.[9]

A. A. Hodge, the son of Charles Hodge and Professor of Systematic Theology at Princeton Seminary, wrote:

A *bona fide* offer of the gospel, therefore, is to be made to all men – 1st. Because the satisfaction rendered to the law is sufficient for all men. 2d. Because it is exactly adapted to the redemption of all. 3d. Because God designs that whosoever exercises faith in Christ shall be saved by him. Thus the atonement makes the salvation of every man to whom it is offered objectively possible. The design of Christ's death being to secure the salvation of his own people, incidentally to the accomplishment of that end, it comprehends the offer of that salvation freely and honestly to all men on the condition of their faith. No man is lost for the want of an atonement, or because there is any other barrier in the way of his salvation than his own most free and wicked will.[10]

Robert Lewis Dabney, the leading theological guide of the Southern Presbyterian Church during the 19th century, likewise affirms:

But [Christ's] sacrifice, expiation, is one—the single, glorious, indivisible act of the divine Redeemer, infinite and inexhaustible in merit. Had there been but one sinner, Seth, elected of God, this whole divine sacrifice would have been needed to expiate his guilt. Had every sinner of Adam's race been elected, the same one sacrifice would be sufficient for all. We must absolutely get rid of the mistake that expiation is an aggregate of gifts to be divided and distributed out, one piece to each receiver, like pieces of money out of a bag to a multitude of paupers. Were the crowd of paupers greater, the bottom of the bag would be reached before every pauper got his alms, and more money would have to be provided. I repeat, this notion is utterly false as applied to Christ's expiation, because it is a divine act. It is indivisible, inexhaustible, sufficient in itself to cover the guilt of all the sins that will ever be committed on earth. This is the blessed sense in which the Apostle John says (1st Epistle ii. 2): "Christ is the propitiation (the same word as expiation) for the sins of the whole world."[11]

The affirmation of an unlimited sufficiency in Christ's atoning work is further affirmed by Henry C. Fish in *The Baptist Scriptural Catechism* of 1850 where it contains the following exchange:

Q. Did the atonement, in its saving design, embrace more than the elect?

A. The elect only; for whatever he designed he will accomplish, and he saves only "his people from their sins." Matt. i. 21.

Q. And yet, was it not in its nature of sufficient value for the salvation of all mankind?

A. It was; and hence God is said to have "sent his Son into the world that the world through him might be saved." John iii.17. Heb. ii.9. John i.29. II Cor.v.14-20. I Tim.ii.6. I John ii.2.[12]

Conclusion

Why is it important to understand the sufficiency of the death of Jesus Christ to save all men? I believe there are two very important reasons.

First, the sufficiency of Christ's death gives us an accurate understanding of the character of God. If we believe that Christ died *only* for the elect, and makes no provision at all for the non-elect, we would have no choice but to see God as heartless and unfeeling towards the majority of the human race. Some Christians believe that God has nothing but hatred in His heart towards the non-elect. However, when we understand that Christ in His death offered Himself as a sufficient atonement for all men, and sincerely invites all men to come to Him to receive life, we can begin to understand those passages of Scripture which declare, "As I live! I take no pleasure in the death of the wicked, but rather that the wicked turn from his way and live. Turn back, turn back from your evil ways! Why then will you die, O house of Israel?" (Ezekiel 33:11); "The Lord is good to all, and His mercies are over all His works" (Psalm 145:9); and "God desires all men to be saved and to come to the knowledge of the truth" (1 Timothy 2:4). Jesus Himself declared to the unbelieving religious leaders of His day, "O Jerusalem, Jerusalem, who kills the prophets and stones those who are sent to her! How often I wanted to gather your children together, the way a hen gathers her chicks under her wings, and you were unwilling" (Matthew 23:37).

Surely, these passages of Scripture indicate a general benevolence, kindness, love and compassion of God towards all men. Because of this genuine pity, God does not desire the sinner's destruction, but rather that he would turn and live. We know, of course, that this desire of God for every man's salvation is not equal to His sovereign purpose to save the elect. Though difficult for us to understand, Scripture indicates that God desires the salvation of all men, yet has not decreed in His infinite wisdom to save all men. Rather, He has purposed in His sovereignty to infallibly save His elect, while allowing the rest to pursue their own sinful lusts to their own destruction.

Though we may want to eat a hot fudge sundae, we may choose not to because we have a stronger desire to lose weight. In that case, we have real desires which we have the power to fulfill, but choose not to fulfill in order to accomplish a greater purpose. Likewise, theologian R. L. Dabney illustrates this truth by pointing out that though General George Washington had real and profound compassion for Major Andre who had committed high treason against the U.S. government, he still resolutely signed his death warrant.[13] Surely, if human beings sometimes act contrary to their legitimate desires because of the higher principles of justice and wisdom, it should not be difficult for us to imagine that our infinitely complex God does also.

Secondly, the sufficiency of Christ's death for all men enables us to extend a sincere gospel offer of salvation to all men. Christ has commanded us to preach the gospel to all creation (Mark 16:15); declared that whoever believes in Him shall not perish but have everlasting life (John 3:16); and that his servants are to proclaim, "Come, for everything is ready now" (Luke 14:17). If Christ in His death has not made salvation possible for the non-elect, how can we urge them to believe on Christ in order to be saved? Hypothetically speaking, even if they did believe, they could not be saved, for Christ, according to this view, did not atone for their sins. Therefore, if Christ's atoning work did not make salvation possible for the non-elect, we are left with the untenable position that God commands all men to come to Christ to be saved, even though if they did come, there would be no salvation provided for them. If Christ died strictly for the elect *alone*, then sinners can never know whether Christ died for them or not until *after* they have believed. In that case, there are no objective grounds for a sinner to come and trust in Christ for salvation, because he can't know whether there is any salvation available to him until *after* he has been converted. Surely, this is to reverse the order. First we see that Christ is an all-sufficient Savior. Then, we come to Him in faith relying upon Him alone for salvation.

We will never be completely free to urge all men to come to Christ for salvation until we believe that His death is sufficient for all men, elect or not. With that understanding we can go forth and declare that God was in Christ reconciling the world to Himself and beg sinners to be reconciled with God (2 Corinthians 5:19-20). We can invite, plead, and entreat men and women to come to Christ, assuring them that a full and free salvation is waiting for them. We can lift up our voices and cry out, "Come, for everything is now ready!" However, without this conviction, we will find ourselves hedging the gospel invitation by saying, "if you come to Christ you can know that

He died for you." Or, worse yet, we might decide that the gospel should not be offered to all men, but only to those sinners who give some evidence that they are elect by being *sensible* of their sin. Rather than giving us freedom and boldness in preaching the gospel to all, this would quench our zeal for the lost. If we are to take the gospel to all men, it is important to see Christ's death as sufficient to save all men.

NOTES:

1. The word "atonement" in chapters 4, 5, and 6 is not used in its technical New Testament sense as "at-one-ment" or an actual reconciliation between a sinner and God, for this takes place only when He is united to Christ in regeneration by the work of the Holy Spirit. Rather, I am using the word in its comprehensive sense as the death of Christ as satisfaction for sin in order to procure forgiveness and salvation. Under the umbrella of the word "atonement" we can speak of redemption, reconciliation, propitiation, and expiation.

2. John Calvin, *Calvin's New Testament Commentaries, The Gospel According to St. John, Part One* (Grand Rapids: Eerdmans, 1988) 32.

3. John Charles Ryle, *Expository Thoughts on the Gospels, Vol. 3*, (Grand Rapids, Baker: 1990) 156.

4. Calvin, *John, Part One*, 73, 74.

5. John Calvin, *Institutes of the Christian Religion, III, 1.1* (Philadelphia: The Westminster Press, 1960) 537.

6. Philip Schaff, *The Creeds of Christendom, Vol. 3, The Evangelical Protestant Creeds* (Grand Rapids: Baker, 1983) 586.

7. Edwards, *Works, Vol. 2,* 111.

8. John Newton, *The Works of John Newton, Vol. 4* (Carlisle, Pennsylvania: Banner of Truth, 1985) 193-194.

9. Charles Hodge, *Systematic Theology abridged edition* (Grand Rapids: Baker, 1988) 388-389.

10. A. A. Hodge, *Outlines of Theology,* (Carlisle, Pennsylvania: Banner of Truth, 1972) 420.

11. Robert Lewis Dabney, *The Five Points of Calvinism,* (Harrisonburg, Virginia: Sprinkle Publications, 1992) 61.

12. Henry C. Fish, *The Baptist Scriptural Catechism, 2 vols.* (New York: Edw. H. Fletcher, 1850), 2:52.

13. Robert Lewis Dabney, *Discussions of Robert Lewis Dabney, Vol. 1,* (Carlisle, Pennsylvania: Banner of Truth, 1967) 284-285.

Chapter 5

Redeeming Grace:
The Design of the Atonement

Not only does Christ's death appear glorious when we understand that it is sufficient for all men, but it appears even more glorious when we understand its sovereign design. Though the death of Jesus Christ was sufficient to save all men, it was sovereignly designed to infallibly save the elect alone. When it comes to the sufficiency of the cross, it was unlimited. When, however, it comes to the saving design and intention of God in the cross, it was limited to the elect.

The Atonement Was Designed
To Save The Elect

The sufferings and death of Jesus Christ were God's means of bringing to pass His purpose of election. Having chosen a great number of persons to salvation before the foundation of the world, He still needed to send His Son to secure their salvation. Thus, Christ was born, lived, suffered, died, and rose again in order to save His people from their sins (Matthew 1:21).

The Scriptures teach that Christ came into the world to represent a particular group of people. Jesus repeatedly spoke of those that the Father had given Him. "For I have come down from heaven, not to do My own will, but the will of Him who sent Me. And this is the will of Him who sent Me, that of *all that He has given Me* I lose nothing, but raise it up on the last day" (John 6:38-39). "Father, the hour has come; glorify Thy Son, that the Son may glorify Thee, even as Thou gavest Him authority over all mankind, that to *all whom Thou hast given Him*, He may give eternal life" (John 17:2).

These same people are sometimes referred to as His sheep. Jesus taught that they would hear the voice of their Shepherd and follow Him. He, as their Shepherd-Savior, would lay down His life in order to give them eternal life, so that they would never perish. "I am the good shepherd; the good shepherd lays down His life for *the sheep*" (John 10:11). "*My sheep* hear My voice, and I know them, and they follow Me; and I give eternal life to them, and they shall never perish; and no one shall snatch them out of My hand" (John 10:27-28). Paul refers to these people as God's flock that Christ purchased with His own blood. "Be on guard for yourselves and for *all the flock*, among which the Holy Spirit has made you overseers, to shepherd the church of God which He purchased with His own blood" (Acts 20:28).

In other Bible passages, these people are referred to as "the many." "By His knowledge the Righteous One, My Servant, will justify *the many*, as He will bear their iniquities" (Isaiah 53:11); "just as the Son of Man did not come to be served, but to serve, and to give His life a ransom for *many*" (Matthew 20:28); "for this is My blood of the covenant, which is poured out for *many* for forgiveness of sins" (Matthew 26:28); "so Christ also, having been offered once to bear the sins of *many*, shall appear a second time for salvation without reference to sin, to those who eagerly await Him" (Hebrews 9:28).

In other passages these people are called His church. "Be on guard for yourselves and for all the flock, among which the Holy Spirit has made you overseers, to shepherd *the church of God* which He purchased with His own blood" (Acts 20:28). "Husbands, love your wives, just as Christ also loved *the church* and gave Himself up for her" (Ephesians 5:25).

As we can readily see, though Christ's death was sufficient for all, He had a specific group of people in mind when He went to the cross. These people – referred to as those given Him by the Father, the many, the sheep, and the church – are the ones He came to save. They are those chosen in Him from before the foundation of the world (Ephesians 1:4). They are those who will be saved according to God's own purpose and grace granted them in Christ Jesus from all eternity (2 Timothy 1:9). They are those who have been appointed to eternal life (Acts 13:48).

Christ's death can be likened to an elephant gun. An elephant gun is a very powerful firearm, sufficient to kill an elephant, the largest of all land animals on the earth today. Yet, it can be used to kill something as small as a mouse if aimed properly. Likewise, Christ's death is capable of saving the whole world, yet God wasn't aiming at the world. He was aiming at those He had chosen for salvation from before the foundation of the world.

The Atonement Secured the Saving Work of the Holy Spirit

Though the death of Christ makes the salvation of all men possible because of its inherent sufficiency, it makes the salvation of the elect certain because of its inherent efficacy. The Scriptures teach that the saving work of the Holy Spirit was purchased and secured by Christ in His death. Thus, the regenerating work of the Holy Spirit, resulting in faith, repentance, justification, sanctification, perseverance, and glorification all flow from the work of Christ at Calvary.

In Paul's epistle to Titus he writes, "He saved us, not on the basis of deeds which we have done in righteousness, but according to His mercy, by *the washing of regeneration and renewing by the Holy Spirit, whom He poured out upon us richly through Jesus Christ our Savior*" (Titus 3:5-6).

Herein lies the particularity of the atoning work of Jesus Christ. This text makes clear that the regenerating and renewing work of the Holy Spirit takes place by virtue of Christ's death. Yet, the Holy Spirit is given in saving efficacy only to God's elect. Therefore, though Christ died for all men, He did not die equally for all. He purchased some things for all men, but all things for some men. Christ, in His death, accomplished something more for the elect than He did for the non-elect. Though He made the salvation of all men possible, He made the salvation of the elect certain, by purchasing for them the all-powerful influences of the Holy Spirit, who would convict, regenerate, indwell, seal, and sanctify them. We shall have occasion to speak more about the Spirit's work in a succeeding chapter. Suffice it to say, that Christ infallibly secured the salvation of all those given to Him by the Father by securing for them the saving work of the Holy Spirit, who would effectually apply Christ's atonement to them.

This same truth comes out also in Acts 5:30-31 where Peter declares to the members of the Sanhedrin, "The God of our fathers raised up Jesus, whom you had put to death by hanging Him on a cross. He is the one whom God exalted to His right hand as a Prince and a Savior, to grant repentance to Israel, and forgiveness of sins." Notice that because of Christ's death, resurrection, and ascension He is now a Prince and a Savior who grants repentance and forgiveness of sins. In other words, by virtue of His death, Christ has the right and ability to apply the fruits of His death. And, not only does He possess that right, but He exercises that right in sovereign majesty. Not only does Christ bestow forgiveness of sins, but He also grants the means by which we receive that forgiveness – repentance (Acts 2:38). Thus, we see again that Christ by His death did much more than merely make salvation possible for all. He made salvation certain for His elect by obtaining the ability to apply His redeeming work to their lives through the Holy Spirit.

Further, the apostle Paul as part of his argument to prove nothing is able to separate a true believer from the saving and sustaining love of God declares, "He who did not spare His own Son, but delivered Him up for us all, how will He not also with Him freely give us all things?" (Romans 8:32). Here Paul is arguing from the greater to the lesser. Since God has already paid the greatest possible price when He delivered up His Son to death, surely He will not withhold any lesser gifts, but, with Christ, also freely give us all things. A couple of observations are in order from this text. First, the context restricts the "us all" Christ was delivered up for to the elect. Paul is speaking of those who love God (Romans 8:28), those who were foreknown, predestined, called, justified and are sure of being glorified (Romans 8:29-30). Furthermore, they are expressly declared the elect in the very next verse, "Who will bring a charge against God's elect?" (Romans 8:33). Secondly, the "all things" Paul says God will freely give to those He delivered His Son up to death for, must refer to the various aspects of the application of redemption: calling, justification, preservation, and glorification (Romans 8:30, 38-39). Since God does not give these blessings to all men, Christ must not have been delivered up for all men in the same way. Although Christ died to make salvation possible for all, we see here that He died to make salvation absolutely certain for the elect.

In Titus 2:14 the apostle Paul points to this same truth when he declares that Jesus Christ "gave Himself for us, that He might redeem us from every lawless deed and purify for Himself a people for His own possession, zealous for good deeds." Just a few verses earlier, in Titus 2:11, Paul affirmed that the "grace of God has appeared, bringing salvation to all men." Clearly, Paul in this passage maintains that Christ's atoning death which brings salvation is made available and offered to all men who hear the gospel, and speaks of its inherent sufficiency to save all. However, three verses later, Paul speaks of the particular design of the atonement when He says that Christ gave Himself for us "that He might redeem us from every lawless deed and purify for Himself a people for His own possession."

Here we have God's sovereign intention in Christ's atonement. Having offered Himself as a satisfaction for sin, Christ now has the right and ability to sovereignly apply that atonement by redeeming and purifying a definite people. These people are described as "a people for His own possession" – an expression which is borrowed from Exodus 19:5 where God depicts Israel, His chosen people under the Old Covenant, as "My own possession among all the peoples." Paul borrows this language, and applies it to the Church, God's chosen covenant people of the New Covenant. Thus, though Christ's atoning sacrifice is sufficient for and available to all men, its design was to secure the eternal salvation of all God's chosen people. The risen Christ now applies this salvation to His chosen people in a way of covenant faithfulness.

The authors of the Canons of the Synod of Dort affirmed the particularity of the intention of Christ in His death to save His elect by purchasing for them the gifts of the Holy Spirit when they wrote:

> For this was the sovereign counsel and most gracious will and purpose of God the Father that the quickening and saving efficacy of the most precious death of His Son should extend to all the elect, for bestowing upon them alone the gift of justifying faith, thereby to bring them infallibly to salvation; that is, it was the will of God that Christ by the blood of the cross, whereby He confirmed the new covenant, should effectually redeem out of every people, tribe, nation, and language, all those, and those only, who were from eternity chosen to salvation and given to Him by the Father; that He should confer upon them faith, which, together with all the other saving gifts of the Holy Spirit, He purchased for them by His death; should purge them from all sin, both original and actual, whether committed before or after believing; and having faithfully preserved them even to the end, should at last bring them, free from every spot and blemish, to the enjoyment of glory in His own presence forever.[1]

Andrew Fuller, an English Particular Baptist of the 18th and 19th century, points to this same glorious truth by affirming:

It is allowed that the death of Christ has opened a way whereby God can consistently with his justice forgive any sinner whatever who returns to him by Jesus Christ. It is necessary to our salvation that a way and a highway to God should be opened: Christ is such a way, and is as free for any sinner to walk in as any highway whatever from one place to another; but, considering the depravity of human nature, it is equally necessary that some effectual provision should be made for our walking in that way. We conceive that the Lord Jesus Christ made such a provision by his death, thereby procuring the certain bestowment of faith, as well as all other spiritual blessings which follow upon it . . . Herein consists the particularity of redemption.[2]

Likewise, James P. Boyce, the principal founder of the first Southern Baptist Seminary in Kentucky in the mid 19th century, writes:

That same death however, secures salvation to the Elect, because by it Christ also obtained for them those gracious influences by which they will be led to comply with the conditions.[3]

Robert Lewis Dabney concurs:

Some sinners (i.e., elect), receive from God gifts of conviction, regeneration, faith, persuading and enabling them to embrace Christ, and thus make His atonement effectual to themselves; while other sinners do not. But these graces are a part of the purchased redemption, and bestowed through Christ. Hence His redemption was intended to affect some as it did not others.[4]

The Atonement Is In Perfect Harmony With Election And Calling

If God the Father has chosen to save a people from all eternity, and God the Spirit applies salvation to these very ones (2 Thessalonians 2:13), then it must follow that God the Son had these same persons in view when He went to the cross. Do the three persons of the Trinity work together to accomplish the same purpose, or do they have cross purposes from one another? In other words, has the Father elected a people, Christ died with the intention of saving all men, while the Holy Spirit only regenerates those the Father has elected? We ought not entertain such unworthy thoughts of God as to imagine the members of the Trinity working towards different goals. Jesus said that He came down from heaven not to do His own will, but the will of Him who sent Him (John 6:38).

The Scriptures indicate that God has a universal love of benevolence, pity, and compassion for all His creatures (Ezekiel 33:11; John 3:16; Titus 3:4), while at the same time, a particular saving love towards His elect (Ephesians 1:4-5; 2:4; Romans 9:21-25). Moreover, God extends a universal call to all men who hear the gospel to repent and believe (Matthew 22:14), while at the same time, issues a particular saving call which draws the elect effectually to Christ (Romans 8:30). Furthermore, God grants universal (common) grace to all men (Matthew 5:43-48), while bestowing saving grace upon His elect alone (Ephesians 2:4-5). Why then should it surprise us to find that not only is there a universal sufficiency in Christ's death for all, but there is also a particular design to render the salvation of the elect certain?

This truth becomes clear when we recognize that the salvation of sinners is the result of an eternal arrangement between the three persons of the Godhead. Before the foundation of the world, the Father, Son, and Holy Spirit agreed upon the terms of this arrangement. God the Father chose a great number of the human family and gave them to Christ as the reward of His obedience and suffering (Ephesians 1:4; John 17:2). God the Son agreed to secure the salvation of these persons by His perfect obedience and substitutionary death (John 6:38-39; Isaiah 53:10-12). Finally, God the Holy Spirit agreed to quicken these elect sinners, make them alive together with Christ, and effectually apply the salvation purchased for them by Jesus Christ.[5]

Conclusion

When a believer grasps the truth that Christ came with a definite design to secure his salvation, he will appreciate the cross like never before.

Imagine a Christmas party at work where the employees exchange gifts with one another. Each employee purchases a gift, wraps it, and puts it under the decorated tree, but doesn't know who will end up receiving it. Because I am wealthy and money is no object, I buy an expensive diamond ring, wrap it, and place it under the tree. One of the ladies present at the party happens to pick the gift which I had wrapped. When she unwraps her present she is stunned to see the beautiful diamond ring inside, but it does not touch her deeply emotionally, because she knows that the person who gave the gift did not have her in mind when buying it.

Now, let us change the situation a little bit. Let us suppose that I want to buy a special Christmas gift for my wife to show her just how much I love her. I scrimp and save throughout the year. In order to get the amount of money needed, I go to the bank and empty our savings account. When she is out with her girlfriends, I secretly shop with her in mind and pick out a ring I know she will love. Then, in anticipation of her face lighting up with joy as she opens the gift, I carefully wrap the box and place it under the tree.

Which person, do you suppose, will have a deeper appreciation for the gift — the lucky fellow employee, or the dearly loved and cherished wife? Which one will be overwhelmed by my gift? Of course it will be the one I had particularly in mind when I made such a great sacrifice of love. Likewise, the stupendous nature of God's grace is showcased when we realize that Christ died in particular for His elect. If Jesus did not die for anyone in particular, but left the results of His cross-work to those who would happen to choose Him, His love would not be nearly as precious and meaningful as it is when you know that He had you particularly in mind when He went to the cross. The Bible teaches that, if we are Christians, Jesus Christ had us specifically in mind when He died to purchase our salvation. Christ was not dying for a nameless, faceless blob of humanity in hopes that someone out there would benefit from it by choosing Him of their free will. Rather, He was dying to purchase a full and free salvation for His people, including the gifts of faith and repentance.

The truth of God's sovereign design in the death of Christ not only fills us with gratitude and wonder that He had us specifically in mind when He offered Himself in sacrifice upon the cross. It also gives us great confidence that God's purposes are sure, and can in no way be frustrated. If Christ in His death had no absolute intention to save any particular persons, it is possible that heaven would be left unpopulated. If Christ died for all men equally, leaving the results of who would benefit from His death to the sinner's fickle will, how could we have any confidence that anyone would be saved? We could send our missionaries to foreign lands, hoping against hope, that someone would decide to follow Christ, yet not know whether anyone would be saved. However, when we realize that Christ went to the cross to purchase His elect from every tribe and tongue and people and nation (Revelation 5:9), we can send out missionaries into all the earth, knowing that Christ has made certain the salvation of a great multitude which no man can number (Revelation 7:9). Their salvation is certain and must infallibly come to pass. Furthermore, we understand how Jesus could say, "I *have* other sheep, which are not of this fold; I *must* bring them also, and they *shall* hear My voice; and they *shall* become one flock with one shepherd" (John 10:16).

NOTES:

1. Schaff, *Creeds*, 587.

2. Andrew Fuller, *The Works of Andrew Fuller, Volume 3* (Harrisonburg, Virginia: Sprinkle Publications, 1988) 2:489.

3. James P. Boyce, *Abstract of Systematic Theology* (Escondido, California: Dulk Christian Foundation, 1887) 340.

4. Robert Lewis Dabney, *Systematic Theology,* (Carlisle, Pennsylvania: Banner of Truth, 1985) 522.

5. Many Reformed scholars refer to this agreement as "The Covenant of Redemption." Professor John Murray preferred to call it the "Inter-Trinitarian Economy of Salvation." He writes, "It is not necessary to make much of an issue respecting terminology. But it may not be remiss to observe that the term 'covenant' in Scripture refers to temporal administration, and it is

not strictly proper to use a biblical term to designate something to which it is not applied in the Scripture itself. For this reason it is not well, and is liable to be confusing, to speak of this economy in terms of covenant." (*Collected Writings of John Murray, Vol. 2,* Banner of Truth, 130.)

Chapter 6

Redeeming Grace:
The Benefits of the Atonement

～〜◯

The overwhelming nature of God's grace becomes apparent not only as we see its sufficiency for all and its particular design for the elect, but also the rich and precious benefits that accrue to those who believe on Him.

The Death Of Christ Redeems From Sin

To "redeem" means to set free by the payment of a ransom. For us to say that Jesus is our redeemer, is to say that He is our ransomer. Inherent in the concept of redemption are the ideas of deliverance and purchase. We have all read accounts in which a kidnapper steals a wealthy man's child, and demands a ransom to be given by a specific date and time. When the money is given as ransom, the child is set free (at least that is how it is supposed to work!). When we believed in Jesus Christ, we were set free from the curse of the Law, the fear of death, this present evil age, and our former futile lives. Consider the following texts:

Galatians 3:10, 13: "For as many as are of the works of the Law are under a curse; for it is written, 'Cursed is everyone who does not abide by all things written in the book of the law, to perform them.' Christ redeemed us *from the curse of the Law*, having become a curse for us— for it is written, 'Cursed is everyone who hangs on a tree.'" The Bible is clear that all those who seek to be justified by observing the Law, are under its curse. But Christ has set us free from the curse of the Law by becoming a curse for us when He hung upon the cross.

Hebrews 2:14-15: "Since then the children share in flesh and blood, He Himself likewise also partook of the same, that through death He might render powerless him who had the power of death, that is, the devil; and might deliver those who through *fear of death* were subject to slavery all their lives." In this text we are reminded that Christ delivers us from the fear of death. The fear of death arises from the dreaded anticipation that after death we will experience the wrath of God because of our sin. However, because we are assured that Christ bore our sin, and removed God's wrath, we are set free from this paralyzing fear.

Galatians 1:3-4: "Grace to you and peace from God our Father, and the Lord Jesus Christ, who gave Himself for our sins, that He might deliver us out of *this present evil age*, according to the will of our God and Father." Not only did Christ's death deliver believers from the curse of the Law and the fear of death, but also from this present evil age. Christ's death has delivered us from this present evil age through its sanctifying influences. 1 Peter 2:24 says, "He Himself bore our sins in His body on the cross, *that we might die to sin and live to righteousness.*" It is through this dying to sin and living to righteousness that God delivers us out of this present evil age, and separates us unto Himself as His own special people.

Ephesians 1:7: "In Him we have redemption through His blood, *the forgiveness of our trespasses*, according to the riches of His grace." In this text the apostle Paul highlights the fact that Christ's sacrificial death is the means by which we are freed from the punishment due us because of our sins. Christ's death brings forgiveness rather than wrath to those who believe. "To Him who loves us, and *released us from our sins* by His blood" (Revelation 1:5).

1 Peter 1:18-19: "knowing that you were not redeemed with perishable things like silver or gold *from your futile way of life* inherited from your forefathers, but with precious blood, as of a lamb unblemished and spotless, the blood of Christ." Peter affirms that Christ by His death has redeemed us from our futile way of life inherited from our forefathers. Whether Peter's readers were Jews who were ignorant of God's Messiah, or Gentiles whose lives were steeped in superstition and idolatry, their lives were empty. Christ, by His death, set them (and us) free from an empty, futile life, and brought them into an abundant life filled with eternal purpose and meaning.

The Death Of Christ Reconciles To God

As sinners we arrive in this world as God's enemies. Sin is that which produces this great hostility between God and man. The only way that a sinner can have this hostility removed so that he can be the friend of God is to have his sins removed, and the only way his sins can be removed is through the sacrificial death of Jesus Christ. Through faith in Christ, a sinner becomes the friend of God, no longer alienated by wicked works, but brought near to God through the blood of Christ. Consider God's Word:

Romans 5:10: "For if while we were enemies, *we were reconciled to God through the death of His Son*, much more, having been reconciled, we shall be saved by His life." Notice in this text that our reconciliation with God was achieved on the ground of Christ's death. That which separated God and man is sin. By dying for our sins, Christ was able to remove that which caused the enmity, thereby obtaining our reconciliation to God.

Colossians 1:21-22: "And although you were formerly alienated and hostile in mind, engaged in evil deeds, yet He has now *reconciled you in His fleshly body through death*, in order to present you before Him holy and blameless and beyond reproach." Sinners are at war with God. They are God's enemies. In Colossians 1:20 Paul explains that Christ made peace through the blood of His cross. The only way our sins could be removed was for Christ to die for them as our substitute. When He did this, He removed the cause of hostility, and made it possible for us to be at peace with God.

1 Peter 3:18: "For Christ also died for sins once for all, the just for the unjust, *in order that He might bring us to God.*" Before we were saved, we were separate from Christ, alienated from God, and cut off from all hope (Ephesians 2:12). Christ's death, however, paid the penalty our sins deserved, removed the enmity and reconciled us to God.

The Death Of Christ Propitiates God

A propitiation is a sacrifice or payment which removes wrath. For example, let us suppose that you have been shopping, and having finished, walk out to your car to put your groceries away. As you approach, you notice a large dent in the passenger door, as well as a car nearby with a large dent in its front bumper. As you are taking all of this in, a man runs over to you and exclaims, "I'm so sorry! It all happened so fast!

I'll pay for the damages. Here - is this enough?" All the time he is talking, he's putting $100 bills in your hand. Now, your car is only worth $1,000, but he has already placed $2,000 dollars in your hands. At this point, you turn to him and say, "Yes, that's enough. I'm satisfied! I'm happy! Don't worry about that old dent; this will do just fine!" In this illustration he has propitiated you. He has offered a payment which satisfied you and made you happy. In the same way, Jesus Christ offered a sacrifice to His Father which satisfied His justice, and removes His wrath from sinners who turn to Christ in faith. The death of Jesus Christ turns away God's righteous indignation so that He can accept the believing sinner without violating His holy nature. Consider how these texts speak of Christ's work at the cross making propitiation:

Hebrews 2:17: "Therefore, He had to be made like His brethren in all things, that He might become a merciful and faithful high priest in things pertaining to God, *to make propitiation for the sins of the people*." How did Christ make propitiation for the sins of the people? The answer lies three verses earlier where the Scripture states, "Since then the children share in flesh and blood, He Himself likewise also partook of the same, that *through death* He might render powerless him who had the power of death, that is, the devil." Christ propitiated God by bearing the wrath that our sins deserved.

1 John 4:10: "In this is love, not that we loved God, but that He loved us and sent His Son *to be* *the propitiation for our sins.*" When Scripture writers speak of the Father "sending" the Son, they are referring to the whole redemptive mission of Jesus Christ which culminated in His death and resurrection. When the Father sent the Son on a mission to save His people, He did so by becoming a wrath-averting sacrifice for their sins.

Romans 3:24-26: "being justified as a gift by His grace through the redemption which is in Christ Jesus; whom God displayed publicly *as a propitiation in His blood* through faith. This was to demonstrate His righteousness, because in the forbearance of God He passed over the sins previously committed; for the demonstration, I say, of His righteousness at the present time, that He might be just and the justifier of the one who has faith in Jesus." Paul explains in this passage that Christ became a propitiatory sacrifice in His blood. That is to say, by the means of His death, Christ has become a propitiation which turns away God's wrath from His believing people.

The Death Of Christ Expiates Sin

Expiation speaks of Christ removing our sins away from (ex) us,[1] and thus, canceling sin.[2] The truth that Christ has removed the sins of believers away from them is found in many places in Scripture. The author of Hebrews states categorically, "but now once at the consummation of the ages He has been manifested *to put away sin* by the sacrifice of Himself" (Hebrews

9:26). John the Baptist cried out in reference to Christ, "Behold, the Lamb of God who *takes away the sin of the world!*" (John 1:29). Furthermore, the apostle John wrote, "And you know that He appeared in order *to take away sins*; and in Him there is no sin" (1 John 3:5). Isaiah prophesies, "He Himself *bore the sin of many*" (Isaiah 53:12), while Peter picks up this theme and writes, "He Himself *bore our sins* in His body on the cross" (1 Peter 2:24).

When Christ died, He purchased forgiveness and justification for all who would believe. This truth is woven like a golden thread throughout the Scriptures. "He made you alive together with Him, having *forgiven us all our transgressions*, having canceled out the certificate of debt consisting of decrees against us and which was hostile to us; and He has taken it out of the way, having nailed it to the cross" (Colossians 2:13-14). "This is the blood of the covenant, which is poured out for many *for forgiveness of sins*" (Matthew 26:28). "In Him we have redemption through His blood, *the forgiveness of our trespasses*, according to the riches of His grace" (Ephesians 1:7). "To Him who loves us, and *released us from our sins* by His blood" (Revelation 1:5). "By His knowledge the Righteous One, My Servant, will *justify the many, as He will bear their iniquities*" (Isaiah 53:11). "Much more then, having now been *justified by His blood*, we shall be saved from the wrath of God through Him" (Romans 5:9).

The doctrine of expiation of sins through the death of Christ is illustrated vividly through the "scapegoat" on the Day of Atonement (Leviticus

16:21-22). On this solemn day, the high priest would lay his hands on the head of a live goat, and confess over it all the sins of the people of Israel. In this way, their sins were symbolically transferred to the head of the live goat. At this point, one of the men of Israel would lead the goat away into a solitary place, and release it never to return again. When the goat had skipped off into the distance, the man would race back into the camp amid great shouts of joy from the sons of Israel. The release of the "scapegoat" into the wilderness each year, signified to the people of Israel that God had taken away their sins never to return again. Likewise, having come to Christ in saving faith, we are confident that He has borne our sins away, never to return to us again (Psalm 103:12; Micah 7:19).

Conclusion

The glory of Christ's work on the cross is highlighted when we see not only that it is sufficient for every individual of Adam's race, sovereignly efficacious for all His elect, but also infinitely precious in its saving benefits. If the cross has redeemed us, then at one time we were slaves to sin. If it has reconciled us, then we at one time were enemies of God and our Lord Jesus Christ. If it has propitiated God, then we at one time were under the wrath of God. And finally, if it has expiated our sins, then at one time the guilt of our sins was upon us. Slaves! Enemies! Deserving of wrath! Full of guilt! That is how the Bible describes us prior to receiving God's rich salvation. If we are free from sin, friends of God, objects of His mercy, and delivered from the guilt of sin which clung to us so tenaciously, it is only because of God's overwhelming grace brought to us through the cross of our Lord Jesus Christ.

Having seen the nature of Christ's atonement, we can begin to truly appreciate God's grace displayed in the cross. Not only were we hopeless and helpless to save ourselves, or to even lift a finger to cooperate with God in our salvation, not only did God decree our salvation from all eternity, but Jesus Christ went to the cross with us particularly in mind and paid the price for every one of our sins. He knew *us* before we were born, and hung between heaven and hell bearing His Father's wrath for *us*. Oh what a glorious thought! Truly His grace is overwhelming. Along with the apostle Paul we can exclaim with wonder, "He loved *me*, and gave Himself *for me*" (Galatians 2:20).

NOTES:

1. R. C. Sproul, *Chosen By God*, (Wheaton, Illinois: Tyndale House Publishers, 1986) 206.

2. Walter A. Elwell, Editor, *Evangelical Dictionary of Theology*, (Grand Rapids, Michigan: Baker Book House, 1984) 888.

Chapter 7

Regenerating Grace

～〇

We come now to the work of the Holy Spirit in our salvation. Just as the Father elected us to salvation, and Christ secured our salvation, so too the Holy Spirit applied Christ's purchased salvation to our lives. We call His initial work in this regard regeneration. To understand regeneration we need look no further than our own experience with dead batteries. We all understand that to regenerate a battery is simply to make it come alive again. In the word regeneration the prefix "re" refers to doing something again, while the word "generate" means to make alive. To regenerate, then, means to make alive again. We were once alive in Adam, our representative. However, when Adam fell, he died, and all of us died in him. But if we are Christians, the Holy Spirit has regenerated us. He has made us alive again in Christ. Let us take a close look at Ephesians 2:4-5 which teaches this thrilling truth:

*But God, being rich in mercy, because of His
great love with which He loved us, even when
we were dead in our transgressions, made us
alive together with Christ (by grace you have
been saved)*

What Did God Do When He Regenerated Us?

What exactly did God do when He regenerated
us? The Bible teaches that He gave us His life, gave
us a new heart, drew us to Christ, and called us to
Christ.

He Gave Us His Life

Our text declares to us that God "made us alive
together with Christ." Now, it must be admitted that
this is exactly what we needed because Ephesians
2:1-3 tells us that we were dead in trespasses and
sins. We were dead to God, cut off from His life, and
alienated from His person. As such, we were under
His wrath and unable to do anything about it. A corpse
cannot bring itself to life, being in a state of complete
helplessness and total inability. Similarly, our great
need was life and that was exactly God's answer.

What does it mean to be made alive together with
Christ? It means that we have experienced a spiritual resurrection. That is what being born again is all
about. Jesus spoke about this spiritual resurrection

in John 5:24-25 when He said, "Truly, truly, I say to you, he who hears My word, and believes Him who sent Me, has eternal life, and does not come into judgment, but *has passed out of death into life.* Truly, truly, I say to you, an hour is coming and now is, when the dead shall hear the voice of the Son of God; and *those who hear shall live.*"

A person who has experienced the new birth has been brought into a whole new world. A newborn baby sees and hears things it has never experienced before. Everything has become new. Likewise, "if any man is in Christ he is a new creature; the old things passed away; behold, new things have come" (2 Corinthians 5:17). The Christian is now able to see, hear, and understand Christ for the first time in his life. He can now please Christ and receive Him. Regeneration can be aptly compared to a blind man receiving sight or a deaf man having his ears unstopped.

When this great change takes place, God implants His very life in the soul of the elect sinner. This is what the Bible means by the gift of eternal life. Eternal life is not just life that goes on forever; it is the very life of God which is eternal in its very essence. Because God has no beginning nor will have any end, His life has no beginning nor end as well. The Bible states clearly that "He who has the Son has the life; he who does not have the Son of God does not have the life" (1 John 5:12). When the Holy Spirit regenerates a sinner, He unites him to Christ in all of His resurrection life. Imagine what it entails to be indwelt by the very life of almighty God! That is exactly what takes place when a person is born again. He is made alive together with Christ.

He Gave Us A New Heart

This new spiritual life that an individual receives at conversion is also described as the receiving of a new heart. This astounding truth is most clearly described in Ezekiel 36:26 where God emphatically states, "Moreover, I will give you a new heart and put a new spirit within you; and I will remove the heart of stone from your flesh and give you a heart of flesh." God affirms in this text that something akin to a spiritual heart transplant takes place in regeneration. God removes the heart of stone and replaces it with a heart of flesh. In fact, this heart of flesh is so radically different from our old heart, that He calls it a "new" heart. This text is depicting the glorious change that takes place in an individual's affections when he is born again. He receives a new nature with new desires and values. He now hates what he once loved, and loves what he once hated. The Christian now takes delight in reading the Bible, fellowshipping with other believers, praying and worshipping God. Similarly, he now hates sin and is grieved when he commits it. God becomes the supreme affection of his new heart.

He Drew Us To Christ

The Bible refers to our new birth in other language as well. Sometimes it refers to this saving change as God "drawing" us. In the words of our blessed Lord, "No one can come to Me, unless the Father who sent Me draws him; and I will raise Him up on the last day. It is written in the prophets, 'and they shall all be taught of God.' Everyone who has heard and learned from the Father, comes to Me" (John 6:44-45). The first thing that must be noted about this assertion is that Jesus uses a universal negative. He says "no one" can come to Him unless the Father draws him. These words allow for no exceptions. Jesus is stating in the most dogmatic language that it is absolutely impossible for anyone to come to Him unless He is drawn by God.

It should be noted, further, that Jesus said, "no one *can* come to Me," not "no one *may* come to Me." The word "can" is a word denoting ability, whereas the word "may" denotes permission. All men are permitted and invited to come to Christ for salvation, but the sobering truth is that of themselves, none can. Coming to Christ speaks of exercising saving faith in Him as Savior, and feasting on Him as the Bread of Life come down from heaven (John 6:35). The unregenerate man cannot do this, because his unrenewed heart will not allow him to. His heart loves sin more than Christ. His greatest desire is to seek his own will and glory rather than the will and glory of Christ. Before he can flee to Christ in saving faith, God must change his heart and affections. This God does in regeneration as He draws him to the Savior.

It is commonly taught today that when God draws the sinner, He merely beckons and woos him to Christ, but it is ultimately up to the sinner to exercise his own free will in order to be saved. Further, it is affirmed that the sinner can resist this drawing of God and be eternally lost.

It is interesting, however, to note how the New Testament uses the Greek word translated as "draw." The word is used of Peter drawing his sword out of his scabbard (John 18:10) and hauling a net containing 153 fish to land (John 21:11), of Paul and Silas dragged into the market place before the authorities (Acts 16:19), and of the rich dragging the poor into court (James 2:6). True, there is resistance in every case, but there is not a single example in the New Testament's use of this word, where the resistance is successful. In every case the drawing power is triumphant. The sword is withdrawn, the fish get to shore, Paul and Silas are dragged before the magistrate, and the poor are brought before the court. In fact, the Greek word is usually translated "drag" or "haul" in the New American Standard Bible. The word carries the meaning "to compel by irresistible superiority."

By saying that this drawing of God is irresistible, I do not want to be misunderstood to be affirming that sinners do not resist the outward call of God in the gospel. Not only do they resist, they must by their very natures resist God's call. In fact, they will continue to resist God's summons to their dying breath unless God's drawing power exerts greater influence upon them than their own sinful nature. The drawing of God must be more powerful than the sinner's resistance, or he is eternally doomed. This drawing proves to be irresistible simply because it destroys the disposition in the sinner to resist, by changing his heart and affections.

Notice also from our text in John 6:44-45 how God draws men. If it is true, as Jesus says it is, that no one can come to Him except those who are drawn by the Father, and that everyone who has heard and learned from the Father comes to Him, then it becomes apparent that the way God draws the elect is by opening their ears to hear His voice and teaching them. By nature all men are spiritually deaf to God's voice, but God in drawing the elect, graciously enables them to hear His voice. As their ears are opened to His voice, He personally teaches them. Just as Jesus could say to Peter, "Blessed are you, Simon Barjona, because flesh and blood did not reveal this to you, but My Father who is in heaven" (Matthew 16:17), so it is true of all God's children. God Himself personally gives them a life-changing revelation of Jesus Christ. After laying bare our rebellious hearts to see the ugliness of our sin and wretchedness before the all holy God, the Holy Spirit shows us the beauty and glory of Christ, so that we come to Him as empty handed beggars to receive salvation.

He Called Us To Christ

Another word used to describe this wondrous work God does in our lives is "calling." It must be admitted that on a few occasions the Bible uses the word "calling" to refer to a call of God which is not answered. This is the gospel call. Whenever the gospel is preached, this call to repentance and faith goes out. This outward call will always be refused if it is not accompanied by an inward call of the Holy Spirit. We see this call in Matthew 22:14 where Jesus says, "Many are called, but few are chosen." This call is insufficient to save, but sufficient to leave men without excuse.

However, the great majority of the time the New Testament authors refer to God's call, they are speaking of something far different. They are describing the effectual call of God. This call is an inward call spoken directly to the heart, whereas the general call is an outward call spoken to the ear. This effectual call is the irresistible summons of the Holy Spirit. We observe this call in Acts 16:14 where we are told that "a certain woman named Lydia, from the city of Thyatira, a seller of purple fabrics, a worshiper of God, was listening; and *the Lord opened her heart to respond* to the things spoken by Paul." In this case, Paul spoke to a group of women. He was only able to reach Lydia's ears, but God was able to open her heart. When we speak of "effectual" calling, we are describing the call of God which comes with such power that it actually produces God's desired effect - the individual's conversion. Note the following texts carefully in order to see the Biblical teaching on God's effectual call:

Romans 8:30: "and whom He predestined, these He also *called*; and whom He called, these He also justified; and whom He justified, these He also glorified." In this text Paul describes God's unbreakable chain of salvation. This chain begins in God predestining a people to be conformed to the image of Jesus Christ. The chain ends in every one of these same people being glorified together with Christ in heaven, having been perfectly conformed to His image. But how does this transformation of a sinner take place? Paul informs us that every one of those who were predestined are also called. Likewise, every one of those who are called are also justified. Moreover, every one of those justified are also glorified. Every person who begins in God's predestined purpose arrives in glory conformed to Christ's image. No one is lost along the way; likewise, no one is added along the way. That is the meaning of "whom He predestined, *these* He also called; and whom He called, *these* He also justified." Therefore, this call cannot be merely an offer of salvation or invitation to Christ, because most people who receive a gospel invitation are never justified. This text informs us that all who are called are also justified. This call must refer to God's effectual call which actually brings an individual into a state of salvation.

1 Corinthians 1:9: "God is faithful, through whom you were *called into fellowship with His Son,*

Jesus Christ our Lord." Calling in this passage refers to that work of God whereby we are actually brought into a living and vital relationship with Jesus Christ. It cannot be understood as simply a gospel offer. This call does not merely offer us fellowship with Christ, it brings us into fellowship with Christ.

1 Corinthians 1:22-24: "For indeed Jews ask for signs, and Greeks search for wisdom; but we preach Christ crucified, to Jews a stumbling block, and to Gentiles foolishness, but to those who are *the called, both Jews and Greeks, Christ the power of God and the wisdom of God.*" Notice that in this text calling cannot be equated with the mere preaching of the gospel, for the gospel is preached to many who view Christ merely as a stumbling block or foolishness, while those who are called savingly experience Him as the power and wisdom of God. While the larger mass of Jews and Gentiles rejected Christ, a smaller group consisting of "the called" responded in faith to Him. The Biblical explanation for the difference in response in these two groups is that God effectually called His elect, while the others were left in their sin and unbelief.

2 Timothy 1:9: "who has saved us, and *called us with a holy calling*, not according to our works, but according to His own purpose and grace which was *granted us in Christ Jesus from all eternity.*" Notice in this text that God's saving and calling are co-extensive. Those that He calls are those that He saves. Thus, the "calling" referred to in this passage is not simply the wooing of the Holy Spirit which may be resisted. Rather it is a work of God which brings sinners into a state of salvation. Further, the text indicates that both our salvation and our calling were gifts granted us from all eternity.

1 Peter 2:9: "But you are a chosen race, a royal priesthood, a holy nation, a people for God's own possession, that you may proclaim the excellencies of Him who has *called you out of darkness into His marvelous light.*" In this passage we are informed that our calling was *from* something and *to* something. We were called out of the kingdom of darkness where Satan ruled (Acts 26:18), into the kingdom of light where Christ is king (Colossians 1:13). Thus, this call is not merely a gospel offer; rather, it is a divine summons which brings a sinner out of Satan's kingdom where he was a slave of sin, and brings him into Christ's kingdom where he is a servant of righteousness. This calling actually effects a kingdom transfer. Furthermore, this call comes to God's "chosen people" who are "a people for His own possession." Clearly then, this call is not merely an invitation which can be successfully refused.

This wondrous, omnipotent call of God is described beautifully in the Westminster Confession of Faith:

> All those whom God hath predestinated unto life, and those only, He is pleased, in His appointed and accepted time, effectually to call, by His

Word and Spirit, out of that state of sin and death, in which they are by nature, to grace and salvation by Jesus Christ; enlightening their minds, spiritually and savingly, to understand the things of God; taking away their heart of stone, and giving unto them a heart of flesh; renewing their wills, and by His almighty power determining them to that which is good, and effectually drawing them to Jesus Christ; yet so as they come most freely, being made willing by His grace. This effectual call is of God's free and special grace alone, not from any thing at all foreseen in man; who is altogether passive therein, until, being quickened and renewed by the Holy Spirit, he is thereby enabled to answer this call, and to embrace the grace offered and conveyed in it.[1]

Thomas Watson, one of my favorite Puritan authors, describes the effectual call in this way:

There is an inward call, when God with the offer of grace works grace. By this call the heart is renewed, and the will is effectually drawn to embrace Christ. The outward call brings men to a profession of Christ, the inward to a possession of Christ. . . God puts forth infinite power in calling home a sinner to Himself; He not only puts forth His voice but His arm. The apostle speaks of the exceeding greatness of His power, which He exercises towards them that believe. Eph.1:19. God rides forth conquering in the chariot of His gospel; He conquers the pride of the heart, and makes the will, which stood out as a fort-royal, to yield and stoop to His grace; He makes the stony heart bleed. Oh, it is a mighty call!. . . The effectual call is mighty and powerful. God puts forth a divine energy, nay, a kind of omnipotence; it is such a powerful call, that the will of man has no power effectually to resist.[2]

When Did God Regenerate Us?

Our text informs us that God did this "when we were dead in our transgressions." A very important question arises at this point. Was my regeneration something that I did, something that God did, or a little bit of both? Another way to ask the same question is, "Does the sinner choose to be born again?" Does his faith cause God to regenerate him, or does regeneration cause him to believe?

Let us analyze the situation for a moment. The Bible tells us that when we were dead in our transgressions, God made us alive. Faith is a spiritual activity. Someone spiritually dead cannot perform a spiritual activity. He must be given spiritual life before he can perform a spiritual function. Obviously God's life could not have been produced by our faith, for we had no faith. We were dead. When a car has a dead battery the horn cannot sound, the lights cannot shine, and the radio cannot play. In these circumstances a person does not say, "If I can just get my lights to come on, then my battery will be recharged." No, he says, "If I can get my battery recharged, then my lights will come on." When someone who had no interest in Jesus Christ comes to believe in Him with all their heart, we know the battery of his soul has been recharged. Somebody has been fooling around under the hood! What has happened? God has given him new life. He has caused his soul to live.

The clear implication from all of this is that a sinner does not choose to be born again. His faith does not cause God to regenerate him. Rather, God chooses to regenerate the sinner, causing him to repent and believe. Can this be established in any other passages of Scripture? It most definitely can.

John 1:12-13: "But as many as received Him, to them He gave the right to become children of God, even to those who believe in His name, *who were born not of blood, nor of the will of the flesh, nor of the will of man, but of God.*" Here John goes out of his way to assure us that our new birth had nothing to do with us, but everything to do with God's sovereign will.

John 3:8: "*The wind blows where it wishes* and you hear the sound of it, but do not know where it comes from and where it is going; so is everyone who is born of the Spirit." John is here comparing the work of the Holy Spirit to the wind. He declares to us that the wind (the same Greek word translated here as "wind" can also be translated as "Spirit") blows where it wishes. We cannot control where the wind will blow. Neither can we control where the Holy Spirit will blow. He regenerates whom He will.

John 5:21: "For just as the Father raises the dead and gives them life, even so *the Son also gives life to whom He wishes*." Just as a dead man cannot cooperate in his own physical resurrection, so we could not assist in our spiritual resurrection. According to Christ in this text, He and His Father give life to the dead. Further, Christ does so to whom He wishes. Jesus Christ is absolutely sovereign in bestowing spiritual life to those dead in sin. Thus, our choice could not have produced our regeneration, for the text clearly says that the Father and the Son give life to the dead, and then only to those they choose to.

Romans 9:16: "So then it does not depend on the man who wills or the man who runs, but on God who has mercy." In this chapter the apostle Paul is exalting the sovereign grace of God by showing how He has bestowed saving love and mercy on some while hardening others. He shows how God chose Isaac rather than Ishmael to be the one through whom Messiah would come. Further, Paul shows that God set His saving love on Jacob rather than Esau, and did so before either were born and had done anything good or bad. God did this so that His own purpose according to His choice might stand, not because of works, but because of Him who calls. He next reveals that God had spoken to Moses, "I will have mercy on whom I have mercy, and I will have compassion on whom I have compassion." Thus, Paul has amply shown that it does not depend on the man who wills or the man who runs. We did not initiate our new birth. God did not respond to our willing or running.

On the contrary, our new birth depends wholly and entirely on God who has mercy.

James 1:18: "*In the exercise of His will He brought us forth* by the word of truth, so that we might be, as it were, the first fruits among His creatures." James has been teaching in this chapter that God does not tempt anyone, nor can He be tempted by evil. Rather, our temptations arise from our own lusts. We cannot blame God for our sin. On the contrary, God constantly gives good gifts (James 1:17). Then, as an example of these good gifts, James mentions our spiritual birth, the first and greatest blessing we receive from God. The expression "brought us forth" in this text refers to giving birth, and is a reference to our being born again. This passage states that the word of truth (the gospel) is the instrument of our regeneration, while God Himself is the agent of regeneration. Kenneth Wuest, in his Expanded Translation, renders the verse, "In accordance with His deliberate purpose He brought us into being by means of the word of truth, resulting in our being a kind of first fruits of His creatures."[3] Because God deliberately purposed our salvation by electing us before the foundation of the world, He brought us forth (regenerated) us through the gospel. Clearly, it was in the exercise of His will, not ours, that we were brought forth to new life.

1 John 5:1: "Whoever believes that Jesus is the Christ *is born of God*; and whoever loves the Father loves the child born of Him." A more literal translation of this verse reads, "Everyone who believes that Jesus is the Christ, out from God has been born."[4] The tenses of the verbs indicates that whoever is presently believing that Jesus is the Christ has been born of God in the past. The words "is born of God" are in the perfect tense which speaks of a past completed action with continuing results. Thus, everyone who presently believes does so because he has been born of God in the past and continues in that state all the days of his life.

Thus, we have seen that this great change we call regeneration is due to the sovereign will of God alone. It is not a response to our repentance and faith, but is that which causes us to repent and believe. It is a work of God alone. We played no part at all in our regeneration in the same way that Lazarus played no part at all in his resurrection and individuals play no part at all in their physical birth. Lazarus did not choose to be raised from the dead, nor did we choose to be born. These acts were outside of our control.

Another question arises at this point. Can this work of regeneration be resisted? In other words, can a person whom the Holy Spirit is trying to regenerate successfully resist His work and be lost? Probably the best way to answer that question is to reply that the Holy Spirit is not "trying" to regenerate people. He is actually regenerating all His elect. Once He has regenerated them, all desire to resist Him has been removed. By changing their hearts, He has successfully destroyed their disposition to resist Him (Ezekiel 36:25-27). Could Lazarus successfully resist Jesus Christ when He called him forth from the dead? Could we resist being born when our mother's time had come? No, "all that the Father has given Me *shall* come to Me" (John 6:37).

Why Did God Regenerate Us?

Our text in Ephesians 2:4 tells us, "But God, being rich in *mercy*, because of His *great love* with which He loved us . . . by *grace* you have been saved." The apostle Paul is teaching us in this text that the reason the Holy Spirit regenerated us was because of God's love, mercy, and grace. This great love is the same love mentioned in Ephesians 1:4 where Paul writes, "In love, He predestined us to adoption as sons through Jesus Christ to Himself." The love Paul is mentioning in this place is His everlasting, unchanging, sovereign, infinite, and invincible love. By nature God is love, but when He relates to sinners, His love becomes grace and mercy. Our text tells us that God is rich in mercy. That is, He does not give us what we deserve. Mercy is God's love directed to sinners in their wretchedness. In His mercy, God takes away the negative consequences of sin. Our text also tells us, "by grace you have been saved." Just as God's mercy does not allow us to experience what we do deserve, so His grace gives us what we do not deserve. Grace is His love directed toward sinners in their guilt. Grace gives us the positive blessings we have not earned. While mercy pities, grace pardons.

Conclusion

The sovereign work of the Holy Spirit in applying our salvation reveals more of the amazing grace of God. Not only was our salvation decreed from all eternity, and secured for us by the particular redeeming death of Jesus Christ, but it was sovereignly applied by the Holy Spirit when He regenerated us. In fact, the work of Christ at the cross without the work of the Spirit within would not have been enough to save us. A.W. Pink in his classic book, *The Sovereignty Of God*, states:

> Had God done nothing more than given Christ to die for sinners and then sent forth His servants to proclaim salvation through Christ, leaving sinners entirely to themselves to accept or reject as *they* pleased, then *every* sinner would have *rejected*, because at heart every man hates God and is at enmity with Him (Rom.8:7). Therefore the work of the Holy Spirit is needed to bring the sinner to Christ, to overcome his innate opposition, and bring him to accept the provision God has made.[5]

This wondrous work of God's Spirit is due exclusively to His sovereign grace. If we have trusted in Jesus Christ to the saving of our souls, it is not because we came up with a good idea one day. Neither is it because we were smarter or had a softer heart than others. It is because we were appointed to eternal life from before the foundation of the world

(Acts 13:48), redeemed by the precious blood of Christ (1 Peter1:18), and given God's very life by the indwelling Holy Spirit (Ephesians 2:4-5). These blessed truths ought to move us to worship God afresh for His incredible grace.

NOTES:

1. Philip Schaff, *The Creeds of Christendom, Volume III, The Evangelical Protestant Creeds,* (Grand Rapids, Michigan: Baker Books, 1983) 624-625.

2. Thomas Watson, *A Body of Divinity,* (Carlisle, Pennsylvania: The Banner Of Truth Trust, 1985) 222-223.

3. Kenneth S. Wuest, *The New Testament: An Expanded Translation,* (Grand Rapids, Michigan: Eerdmans, 1961) 540.

4. Wuest, *Expanded Translation,* 573.

5. A. W. Pink, *The Sovereignty Of God,* (Carlisle, Pennsylvania: The Banner Of Truth Trust, 1928) 72-73.

Chapter 8

Preserving Grace

B y now we have caught a glimpse of how marvelous the sovereign grace of God is. Nevertheless, there is one last area we need to examine. God's grace would be of little value if it could be lost. What would it matter if we were chosen, redeemed, and regenerated by God, if somehow we could lose our salvation in the end? Thankfully, that is utterly impossible. Romans 8:30 tells us, "and whom He predestined, these He also called; and whom He called, these He also justified; and whom He justified, these He also glorified." If we have been predestined, called, and justified, our ultimate glorification in heaven is as good as done. The Bible teaches us that Christ's sheep are infallibly secure in His hands. His grace will be victorious in their lives. They will overcome all the obstacles that will come against them, until they arrive safely in their Father's home in heaven. To see this important truth, let us take a look at those familiar words in John 10:27-29.

> *My sheep hear My voice, and I know them, and they follow Me; and I give eternal life to them, and they shall never perish; and no one shall snatch them out of My hand. My Father, who has given them to Me, is greater than all; and no one is able to snatch them out of the Father's hand.*

In this passage we find several reasons that Christ's sheep are secure. Let us look at each one in turn.

The Love Of Christ

Jesus said, "My sheep hear My voice and I know them." This phrase "I know them" means more than that Jesus is aware of them. It means that He has an intimate relationship of love with them. It speaks of His affection for His sheep. When the Bible says that Adam knew Eve (Genesis 4:1) it means more than he knew what color of eyes she had! It means he had sexual intercourse (the most intimate of encounters) with her. When Jesus says on Judgment Day, "Depart from Me, I never knew you", He will not mean, "Hey, who are you? Where did you come from? I never knew anything about you!" No, He will mean that He never had an intimate saving relationship with you.

Jesus says that He knows His sheep. He has an intimate loving relationship with each one of them. This is a great reason for security in our relationship with Him, because He has known us in this way from all eternity. Jeremiah 31:3 states, "I have loved you with an everlasting love; therefore I have drawn you with lovingkindness." If God decided to have a loving relationship with us from eternity past, even though He knew there was nothing in us to attract His love, how can there ever be anything in us to make Him withdraw that love? In other words, if there was nothing in me to cause Him to love me, there cannot possibly be anything in me to make Him stop loving me.

The Life Of Christ

Jesus explicitly states, "I give *eternal* life to them." Eternal life, by definition, is everlasting, never-ending life. If a person possesses eternal life, he possesses a life that will never end, and thus, can never be lost. To speak of losing eternal life is a contradiction in terms. If a person can lose this life, it was not eternal; it was temporary. The receiving of this eternal life is the same as being regenerated by the Holy Spirit. It is to receive a spiritual, divine, heavenly life, the very life of God Himself. When a person receives God's life, He is connected to God in the same way that a branch is connected to a vine or a body is connected to a head. In regeneration we are vitally united to Jesus Christ. His life flows into us.

Will Christ be dismembered? Will His body arrive in heaven missing a few fingers and toes? When a man stands in a river, as long as he can keep his nose above water, he cannot drown. Christ our Head is in heaven. Whatever floods come against His people here on earth cannot cause them to perish as long as He is alive in heaven. Jesus Himself will have to be cast into hell before any of His blood-bought people can perish there.

The Gift Of Christ

Jesus clearly says "I *give* eternal life to them." If He gives eternal life, then eternal life is not something that we earn. Our good deeds did not purchase it. Now, if I did not earn eternal life by my good works, it is not possible that I can lose eternal life by my bad works. If God gave me my salvation freely as a gift, will He later change His mind and take it back? The Scripture declares, "the gifts and calling of God are irrevocable" (Romans 11:29).

The Promise Of Christ

Our text emphatically asserts, "And they shall *never perish*." At this point someone is bound to object, "Yes, no one can snatch His sheep out of His hand, but they can jump out by their own free will!" Well, if that is true, then Jesus lied. Jesus said that they shall never perish. If we can jump out of

His hand, we will perish. There are only a handful of things that we are told in the Scriptures that God cannot do, and lying is one of them. "God is not a man that He should lie, nor a son of man, that He should repent. Has He said, and will He not do it? Or has He spoken, and will He not make it good?" (Numbers 23:19). Christ has promised His sheep that they shall never perish. Listen to His emphatic promise in John 6:38-39, "For I have come down from heaven, not to do My own will, but the will of Him who sent Me. And this is the will of Him who sent Me, that of all that He has given Me *I lose nothing, but raise it up on the last day.*"

The Possession Of Christ

Jesus said, "*My* sheep hear My voice." Why did He call them "His" sheep? For the simple reason that His Father had given them to Him. He says in verse 29 "My Father, *who has given them to Me*, is greater than all." When did the Father give these sheep to the Good Shepherd? He gave them to Him in His sovereign decree from before the foundation of the world. These sheep have been His from all eternity. We protect and hold on to valuable gifts that we receive from those we love. Because a woman's wedding ring is important to her, she is very careful to put it in a safe place when she takes it off so that she does not lose it. Likewise, because we are a gift to Jesus from the Father, we can be sure that He will hold onto us to the end.

We are also the possession of Christ because He bought and paid for us. He laid down His life as the price required to purchase us for Himself. Is it conceivable then, that He will neglect us and allow us to perish in the end? If I ordered and paid $10 for a shirt that I had to drive an hour to pick up, I might not bother to pick it up when it arrived. I might reason to myself that fighting the traffic and driving the hour to get to the store would be more of a hassle than sacrificing the money I had spent on the shirt. However, if I had paid $5,000 for an exquisite diamond ring I ordered from the store, you can be sure that I would make whatever effort was necessary to pick it up! Likewise, if Christ went through such great sacrifice and pain to purchase us, surely He will go to whatever lengths are necessary to make sure we remain safe and secure in His hands.

The Power Of Christ

Jesus goes on to say in our text, "No one shall snatch them out of My hand." The hand is the place of power. Imagine yourself in the hands of Christ like someone inside the hands of the giant in Gulliver's Travels. Or, to change the metaphor, think of yourself as one of those sheep hoisted up over the shoulders of the Shepherd as He brings it home to His pasture. In the Old Testament the high priest of Israel had the names of the twelve tribes of Israel engraved upon his shoulders and over his heart as he went into the holy of holies to intercede for the people. Likewise, Christ our High Priest has every one of our names engraved upon his shoulders (the place of omnipotence) as He intercedes for us in heaven. In Isaiah 49:15-16 this truth is strongly asserted, "Can a woman forget her nursing child, and have no compassion on the son of her womb? Even these may forget, but I will not forget you. Behold, I have inscribed you on the palms of My hands; your walls are continually before Me." Augustus Toplady must have had this in mind when he wrote these lyrics:

> My name from the palms of His hands
> eternity will not erase
> Impressed on His heart it remains
> in marks of indelible grace
> Yes, I to the end shall endure,
> as sure as the earnest is given
> More happy, but not more secure,
> the glorified spirits in heaven[1]

When Jesus says that no one will snatch His sheep out of His hand, it implies that His sheep will have many enemies that will try to do just that. We as His sheep face the enemies of our sins, temptations, false teachers, persecutors, adversities, and afflictions. But in spite of the attacks of all these, the hands that laid the foundations of the heavens and the earth and hold all things together hold us. Really, it is not our hold on Christ that ultimately matters, but His hold on us. This is the truth that the apostle Paul celebrates in Romans 8:35-39 when he triumphantly declares, "Who shall separate us from the love of Christ? Shall tribulation, or distress, or persecution, or famine, or nakedness, or peril, or sword? Just as it is written, 'For Thy sake we are being put to death all day long, we were considered as sheep to be slaughtered.' But in all these things we overwhelmingly conquer through Him who loved us. For I am convinced that neither death, nor life, nor angels, nor principalities, nor things present, nor things to come, nor powers, nor height, nor depth, nor any other created thing, shall be able to separate us from the love of God, which is in Christ Jesus our Lord." Thomas Brooks, an English Puritan of the 17th century writes:

> Men and devils are as able, and shall as soon, make a world, dethrone God, pluck the sun out of the firmament, and Christ out of the bosom of the Father, as they shall pluck a believer out of the everlasting arms of Christ, or rob Him of one of His precious jewels.[2]

The Power Of God

Please note that there are two sets of hands grasping us. Not only are we in the hands of our Great Shepherd, the Lord Jesus Christ, but we are also in the hands of God the Father. Jesus tells us in verse 29, "My Father, who has given them to Me, is greater than all; and no one is able to snatch them out of *the Father's hand*." The Father is omnipotent in power. No one can rival Him. Think of it. Our Lord wraps His omnipotent hands around us, and the

Father wraps His almighty hands around Christ's. We are encircled in Christ in God as Paul states in Colossians 3:3, "Your life is hid with Christ in God." If God Himself has pledged to protect us, then we are absolutely secure, for there is no greater power in all the universe. Listen to this great truth stated by Peter in 1 Peter 1:3-5, "Blessed be the God and Father of our Lord Jesus Christ, who according to His great mercy has caused us to be born again to a living hope through the resurrection of Jesus Christ from the dead, to obtain an inheritance which is imperishable and undefiled and will not fade away, reserved in heaven for you, who are *protected by the power of God* through faith for a salvation ready to be revealed in the last time."

The Intercession Of Christ

In addition to the wonderful reasons for our security described in John 10:27-29, the Bible lists some others. One of these reasons is the intercession of our Savior at the right hand of God. This is seen very clearly in Christ's high priestly prayer recorded in John 17.

John 17:9-15: "I ask on their behalf; I do not ask on behalf of the world, but of those whom You have given Me; for they are Yours; and all things that are Mine are Yours, and Yours are Mine; and I have been glorified in them. I am no longer in the world; and yet they themselves are in the world, and I come to You. Holy Father, *keep them in Your name*, the name which You have given Me, that they may be one even as We are. While I was with them, I was keeping them in Your name which You have given Me; and I guarded them and not one of them perished but the son of perdition, so that the Scripture would be fulfilled. But now I come to You; and these things I speak in the world so that they may have My joy made full in themselves. I have given them Your word; and the world has hated them, because they are not of the world, even as I am not of the world. I do not ask You to take them out of the world, but to *keep them from the evil one*" (NASB Updated). In this passage Christ is addressing His Father, not on behalf of the world, but on behalf of those whom His Father had given Him (John 17:9). Jesus expressly asks His Father to keep these chosen ones in His name and from the evil one. Is the Father going to answer this prayer of Christ? Christ Himself said that His Father heard Him always (John 11:42). Furthermore, 1 John 5:14-15 reveals to us that God will hear and answer prayer that is according to His will. Surely, this prayer of Christ's for the Father to keep His chosen ones is according to the Father's will. Therefore, we ought to have no doubt that this prayer that the Father would keep and preserve His people unto the end will be answered.

Hebrews 7:25: "Hence, also, He is *able to save forever* those who draw near to God through Him, since He always lives to make intercession for them." Here the intercession of Christ is given as a reason for His ability to save forever those who draw near to God. The previous context indicates that the Levitical priests were prevented from continuing in their priesthood by death. Christ, however, holds His priesthood permanently because He abides forever in the heavens. Thus, He is able to save His people forever. If Christ could cease to function in His high priestly role at God's right hand, His saints could cease to enjoy their salvation. The truth is, however, that because Christ ever lives to make intercession for them, their salvation is secure. This salvation of Christ is not temporary; rather our text declares that it is "forever." Because the child of God has a Savior in the heavens interceding that all of the blessings acquired by His death and resurrection be granted His people, his salvation is secure.

Luke 22:31: "Simon, Simon, behold Satan has demanded permission to sift you like wheat; but I have prayed for you, that your faith may not fail; and you, when once you have turned again, strengthen your brothers." Satan had asked and received permission to subject Peter to a great strain. His objective was to separate Peter from his faith and loyalty to Christ. Anthony Hoekema has insightfully written:

> In the expression "that your faith may not fail," the verb rendered "fail" is *eklipe*, from *ekleipo*, which means "to come to an end," or "to give out." The English word *eclipse*, in fact, is derived from this verb. Kenneth Wuest, therefore, has caught the flavor of this word when he translates, "that

your faith should not be totally eclipsed." Jesus prayed that Peter's faith might not utterly disappear, might not be wiped out without a trace.[3]

Though Peter did go on to deny the Lord three times, his repentance (weeping bitterly with tears) demonstrates that Jesus' intercession was effective. In Peter we have an example of a believer who sinned grievously against the Lord, but did not utterly forsake Christ because of Jesus' intercession.

Romans 8:33-34: "Who will bring a charge against God's elect? God is the one who justifies; who is the one who condemns? Christ Jesus is He who died, yes, rather who was raised, who is at the right hand of God, who also intercedes for us." The apostle Paul tells his readers in no uncertain terms that it is impossible for any of God's believing people to ever be condemned. This security is not based on their perfect performance, but on Christ's perfect work. This work includes not only His substitutionary death, but His ongoing intercession at God's right hand. Because Christ continually intercedes, His people can never be condemned. Notice further, that the people who are secure are described as "God's elect." If God the Father has chosen His people to everlasting salvation, then it is simply not possible that they will fail to inherit that salvation. Jesus Christ, by His death, resurrection, and intercession makes sure of that.

Surely those who were chosen to salvation by the decree of God in eternity past can never end up in hell. Those who have had all their sins wiped away by the atoning death of Jesus Christ, shall never pay for those same sins in the lake of fire. Those who have experienced a spiritual resurrection in their soul surely will never lose their salvation. No, if the Father has sovereignly decreed our salvation, if the Son has sovereignly secured our salvation, and if the Spirit has sovereignly applied our salvation, then that salvation will stand forever.

The Will Of God

Jesus Christ, in John 6:38-39 declared, "For I have come down from heaven, not to do My own will, but the will of Him who sent Me. And this is the will of Him who sent Me, that of all that He has given Me I lose nothing, but raise it up on the last day." In bold, clear language Jesus informs us that it is God's will that every one of those whom He has given to His Son be raised up and glorified on the last day. In fact, Jesus emphatically asserts that it is His Father's will that He should lose nothing. Can the will of God be thwarted? Can His purposes come to naught? Indeed, the Scripture declares that God works all things after the counsel of His will (Ephesians 1:11). Moreover, the Bible asserts, "He does according to His will in the host of heaven and among the inhabitants of earth; and no one can ward off His hand or say to Him, 'What hast Thou done?'"

(Daniel 4:35). No, if it is the will of God that none of those He has given to Christ in electing grace ever be lost, then we can be sure that none ever will. The will of God shall prevail!

The Attributes Of God

We can be sure that God will preserve His elect safely to their heavenly kingdom, because of His holy character. Consider the security to be found in God's attributes.

The Faithfulness Of God

"Now may the God of peace Himself sanctify you entirely; and may your spirit and soul and body be preserved complete, without blame at the coming of our Lord Jesus Christ. Faithful is He who calls you, and He also will bring it to pass" (1 Thessalonians 5:23-24). Notice in this text that both our initial calling and our final preservation when we shall be presented blameless before Him are ascribed to the faithfulness of God.

The Immutability Of God

"For I, the Lord, do not change; therefore you, O sons of Jacob are not consumed" (Malachi 3:6). The reason God's people are not consumed in His wrath is because He does not change. They surely would be consumed if it were not for His unchanging character. However, once God has purposed to save His people, He will never change His mind.

The Grace Of God:

The Bible from one end to the other proclaims that our salvation is of grace. That is to say, it is of God's free and undeserved favor. If we did not receive our salvation because we earned it or became worthy of it, how can it possibly be that we can do anything to lose it? His grace assures that we are eternally secure.

The Love Of God:

"having loved His own who were in the world, He loved them to the end" (John 13:2). God's love was set upon His chosen people from everlasting (Jeremiah 31:3), and shall never be withdrawn. Indeed, all God's people are beloved in God the Father, and kept for Jesus Christ (Jude 1). Those whom God loves He keeps for His Son.

The Sovereignty Of God:

The sovereignty of God is His absolute rule over His creation. As a potter has the absolute right over the clay to do with it what he will, so God has the absolute right to decide what He will do with His creatures. Once He has decided to make an individual into a vessel of mercy, nothing in all the universe can thwart His sovereign purposes (Romans 9:22-24).

Indeed, note how the authors of the Canons of Dort described the security of the saints in 1619:

> Thus, it is not in consequence of their own merits or strength, but of God's free mercy, that they [the elect] do not totally fall from faith and grace, nor continue and perish finally in their backslidings; which, with respect to themselves is not only possible, but would undoubtedly happen; but with respect to God, it is utterly impossible, since His counsel can not be changed, nor His promise fail, neither can the call according to His purpose be revoked, nor the merit, intercession, and preservation of Christ be rendered ineffectual, nor the sealing of the Holy Spirit be frustrated or obliterated.[4]

Conclusion

If we are Christians, we are blessed indeed. Though we were born into this world dead in our sins and under the wrath of God, we were chosen to salvation by God the Father before the foundation of the world, redeemed by the atoning death of Jesus Christ on Calvary's cross, regenerated by the omnipotent Spirit of God, and are being kept for a salvation ready to be revealed in the last times. Can anything in all the world be more wonderful than that? Oh, how breathtaking is God's sovereign grace!

NOTES:

1. Augustus Toplady, 910.

2. Thomas Brooks, *The Works of Thomas Brooks, Volume 2,* (Carlisle, Pennsylvania: Banner of Truth Trust, 1980) 330.

3. Anthony A. Hoekema, *Saved By Grace,* (Grand Rapids, Michigan: Eerdmans, 1989) 237.

4. Philip Schaff, *Creeds, Vol. 3,* 594.

Chapter 9

Questions Concerning Sovereign Grace

⁓

Needless to say, when I first began to study the subject of God's sovereign grace in the Scriptures, I had many questions and objections that I had to wrestle with. I have included some of those questions below, as well as some answers I have found from my own study.

How Can God Hold Sinners Responsible To Do What They Are Unable To Do?

If all men are in a state of total inability to repent and believe savingly on Christ, an objection naturally arises. How can God hold sinners responsible to do something they are unable to do? On the surface, this sounds like an unanswerable question. However, we must remember that man's inability to come to Christ is his own fault. In the beginning Adam had the ability to either obey or disobey (Ecclesiastes 7:29). His choice to eat of the forbidden fruit plunged him and all his descendants into a condition of slavery to sin, and thus, a state of inability to savingly respond to God's offer of mercy.

Imagine a man who asks for welfare support for his family, because he is not able to take care of their needs. When questioned further, he admits that the reason he is not able to provide for his family is because he has deliberately had his arms amputated, and therefore cannot work. When his situation is looked into even more carefully, it becomes apparent that the reason he has had his arms amputated is because he is lazy and does not want to work. Can this individual justly appeal to the United States government to support him and his family because he is unable to provide for his family? It is his own fault that he cannot provide for his family, because he made the willful and deliberate choice to cut off his arms. Likewise, we are at fault for our inability, for all of us sinned in Adam (Romans 5:12-21). Adam justly represented the entire human race, and God holds all of us responsible for that sin (Romans 5:18).

Not only is man's inability to come to Christ his own fault, but it results from the fact that he lacks the necessary will to come to Christ. In other words he *cannot* come to Christ because he *will not* come to Christ. God does not hold men responsible to do what He has not equipped them to do. For example, God does not hold men responsible to fly, because

He has not given them the necessary equipment to fly. However, God does hold men responsible to repent and believe on Christ, because He has given them everything necessary to do that. God has given them a brain that can think, and a will that can choose. However, the sinner will never use his brain and will to repent and believe until God changes his nature, simply because He does not want to. He loves his sin more than Christ.

The sinner's inability is not *natural*, but rather *moral* and *spiritual*. It is the kind of inability that Joseph's brothers evidenced. "And his brothers saw that their father loved him [Joseph] more than all his brothers; and so they hated him and *could not speak to him on friendly terms*" (Genesis 37:4). The inability of Joseph's brothers to speak on friendly terms did not arise because they did not have mouths, lips, and tongues. Rather, they could not speak to Joseph on friendly terms because they had no heart to do so. They hated him. Likewise, the sinner is unable to believe in Christ, love Christ, and repent of sin, not because God hasn't given him a mind, heart, and will that can do these things, but because his mind, heart, and will are in rebellion to God.

Iain Murray convincingly explains the futility of this argument in his wonderful book, *The Forgotten Spurgeon*:

> Man's spiritual inability is due solely to his sin and therefore it in no way lessens his responsibility. That man must be *able* to believe and repent in order to be responsible for unbelief

and impenitency is a philosophical conception nowhere found in Scripture; in fact it is directly contrary to Scripture because, if responsibility were to be measured by ability, then it would mean that the more sinful a man becomes the less he is responsible![1]

Who ever heard of a judge who would not hold a man responsible for his crime of murder merely because he hated his neighbor so much he was unable to keep from pulling the trigger? No, the Bible teaches that the more sinful (and thus, spiritually impotent) a man is, the more responsible he is before God (Romans 2:5-6).

Isn't Election Based On Foreknowledge?

This argument goes something like this: "In Romans 8:29 and 1 Peter 1:2 the Bible declares that election is based on God's foreknowledge. That means that God knew ahead of time who would choose Him, so He chose them. God has not really made any distinguishing choice between who He has determined to save and who He has not; He has merely decided to endorse man's own free choices." This position is very popular today. In fact, at one time I held it. We desperately want to believe that we are the ones that are calling the shots and in control. But are we? Does this explanation accurately present the truth of God's Word? I believe that this explanation of foreknowledge cannot possibly be correct because of the following reasons:

This Makes Man Sovereign

If God only chose us because He knew ahead of time that we would choose Him, God has not really made a choice at all. He has only approved of our choice of Him. But in contrast with this view, notice Christ's words in John 15:16, "You did not choose Me, but I chose you, and appointed you, that you should go and bear fruit, and that your fruit should remain, that whatever you ask of the Father in My name, He may give to you." If we are sovereign, then God is not. But if God is not sovereign, then He is not God, because there is someone or something with more authority and power in the universe than Him.

This Gives Man Some Credit For His Salvation

If my salvation is based on the right use of my free will, then I will have something to boast about in heaven. I will be able to say to the sinner in hell, "The reason I'm up here and you're down there is because I made the right choice, and you didn't!" But God has devised salvation in such a way that no one will ever be able to boast (1 Corinthians 1:26-31; Ephesians 2:8-9).

This Assumes That Man Seeks After God

The Bible, however, explicitly teaches that man does not seek for God. Romans 3:11 teaches us, "There is none who understands, there is none who seeks for God."

This Makes Salvation A Result Of A Human Work

However, the Bible teaches that faith comes from God as a gift (Ephesians 2:8-9; 2 Peter 1:1; John 6:65; Philippians 1:29; Acts 18:27), not as our contribution to salvation. Those individuals alone who are given the faith to believe are the ones appointed to eternal life (Acts 13:48).

Foreknowledge Is Spoken Of In Connection With A People — Not In Connection With Any Action Which People Perform

Notice how foreknowledge is spoken of in Romans 8:29 "For *whom* He foreknew, He also predestined to be conformed to the image of His Son." The text does not say, "For *what* He foreknew." The simple truth is, that God's foreknowledge refers to His special, saving love that He has determined to set upon His elect. To "know" in Scripture often has the meaning of to "love" (Amos 3:2; Matthew 7:23; John 10:14; 2 Timothy 1:19). Foreknowledge then, means to forelove. God has determined beforehand to specially love certain people.

Doesn't Sovereign Election Make God Unfair?

One of the most often raised objections in regard to divine election is that it is unfair. This objection has two possible meanings. It might imply that election makes God unjust. Justice takes place when God gives a man exactly what he deserves. However, God is never unjust. He always gives man exactly what he deserves. All unregenerate men deserve hell because of their sins. All believers deserve eternal life, not because they are deserving in themselves, but because they are "in Christ" and He is deserving. Christ's merit is put to their account. God's sovereignty is never exercised in condemning men who ought to be saved, but in saving men who ought to be condemned. God does no injustice to those who perish. They receive what they rightly deserve.

The question may be asking, however, if the doctrine of election makes God unfair in the sense that He does not give all men exactly the same privileges. The answer to that question is an emphatic *yes*! God has not chosen to give all men exactly the same privileges. God is the One who decided where we would be born, when we would be born, what parents we would have, what natural gifts we would possess, or whether or not we would hear the gospel. Why is it that I was born in a middle class family in the United States, while others were born in poverty-stricken third world nations? Why was I born in the last half of the 20th century where the gospel is proclaimed in a multitude of churches, on radio, television, and print, while others were born as Philistines hundreds of years before Christ, and never heard the way of salvation? Only God's incomprehensible sovereignty can explain it. God has never told us in His Word that He gives all men exactly the same thing. We will search our Bibles in vain in an attempt to find that God has declared that He is fair. Yes, He is just, but He is not fair. He reserves the right to do as He pleases with His own (Matthew 20:15). We must remember that God is the Potter, and has the right to do what He pleases with His clay (Romans 9:21).

When a wealthy woman decides to adopt two orphans out of an orphanage of one hundred children, no one impugns her character as unfair and cruel because she did not adopt the other ninety-eight. Rather, they commend her for her generosity and kindness. Likewise, when a governor grants a pardon to one man out of ten on death row, it is unthinkable to accuse him of acting wickedly toward the other nine. Those who go on to receive the death penalty, are only getting what they deserve, while the one that is pardoned receives mercy. In like manner, it is the height of human arrogance to shake our fist at God and claim that He is cruel and unfair in not choosing to save every member of the human race. The wonder is not that God does not choose to save everyone. The real wonder is that He would choose to save anyone! Seen in that light, God's sovereign election provides us with material for never-ending praise!

What About The Biblical Teaching On Free Will?

Though I cut my spiritual teeth on the doctrine of man's free will, I have searched my Bible in vain to find any clear evidence that a sinner's will is free in the sense that he has the ability to savingly believe in Christ. The "whoever will" passages do not tell us that sinners have the ability to come to Christ. They merely tell us that if they come they shall never perish but have eternal life (John 3:16; Revelation 22:17). Many people think that free will is the ability to repent and believe on Christ at any time, but as we have already seen, the Scriptures teach the exact opposite. A man becomes willing in the day of God's power (Psalm 110:3). In fact, the phrase "free will" is not found in the Bible, except as a reference to the free will offerings of the Old Testament and to Philemon allowing Onesimus to stay and minister to Paul in jail (Philemon 14). The popular teaching on man's free will is conspicuous by its absence in the pages of our Bible.

An individual will always choose according to his greatest preference. If we gave a pig and a cat a choice between living in a clean house or a mud hole, the pig would choose the mud hole and the cat the clean house every time. Even though the pig is free to choose whatever it wants, it will always want to dwell in a dirty environment over a clean one. This preference is built into the nature of the pig. In order for the pig to prefer to live in a clean house more than a muddy pigpen, it would need to have its "pig nature" replaced with a "cat nature." Likewise, the sinner is free to choose sin or Christ, but as long as he possesses the nature of a sinner, he will always choose sin over Christ. In regeneration, God graciously removes the sinner's heart of stone and gives him a new heart - a heart of flesh (Ezekiel 36:26). He becomes a "new creature" (2 Corinthians 5:17). When God saves a man, he changes his nature so completely that he loves what he once hated, and hates what he once loved. Until God works this change in a man's heart, he *cannot* choose Christ, because he *will not* choose Christ. Indeed, Spurgeon once quipped, "Free-will has carried many souls to hell, but never a soul to heaven yet."[2]

How Can Sovereign Election Be True When So Few Christians Believe It?

Perhaps it is true that a minority of believers today hold to the doctrine of sovereign election, but it has not always been that way. In fact, for the first two hundred years after the Protestant Reformation, this teaching was included in the creeds and confessions of the Reformed, Presbyterian, Baptist, Anglican, and Congregational churches. It can be found in the Belgic Confession (1561), the Heidelberg Catechism (1563), the Thirty-Nine Articles of the Church of England (1563), the Second Helvetic Confession (1566), the Canons of the Synod of Dort (1619), the Westminster Confession of Faith (1647), the Savoy Declaration, the London Confession of Faith (1689), and the New Hampshire Confession (1833). In the 16th, 17th, and 18th centuries, sovereign election was believed and taught by the majority of evangelical believers.

Furthermore, the truth of sovereign election has been believed and taught by great men of God throughout church history including Augustine, Martin Luther, John Calvin, John Knox, Hugh Latimer, William Tyndale, John Owen, John Bunyan, Matthew Henry, George Whitefield, Jonathan Edwards, David Brainerd, Isaac Watts, John Newton, William Carey, Robert Murray McCheyne, Charles Haddon Spurgeon, Arthur Pink, and Martyn Lloyd-Jones, among others.

Doesn't The Bible Say That God Is Not Willing For Any To Perish?

Yes, the Scripture declares in 2 Peter 3:9, "The Lord is not slow about His promise, as some count slowness, but is patient toward you, not wishing for any to perish but for all to come to repentance." I believe the key to understanding this text is found in those two words "toward you." Who is the "you" God is patient toward? We find in 2 Peter 1:1 that Peter was writing to "those who have obtained a faith of the same kind as ours, by the righteousness of our God and Savior, Jesus Christ." In other words, Peter is saying that God is patient toward His elect, not wishing for any (of them) to perish, but for all (of them) to come to repentance.

This text should not be understood to mean that Christ's second coming has been delayed because God does not want any to perish. The truth is, the longer Christ waits to return, the more people *will* perish. If God didn't want anyone to perish, the best thing He could have done is sent Christ back in the 1st century. That way, billions of people would not have lived and died, the vast majority of whom perished because of unbelief. Rather, the reason that Christ has not returned yet is that He is not willing for any of His elect to perish, but is waiting for all of them to come to repentance. When the final elect soul has been brought into Christ's kingdom, then He will return.

Won't Belief In Sovereign Election Put Out The Fire Of Evangelism?

Many people think that if they believed in sovereign grace they would never witness to a lost person again. Why should they? The elect will be saved whether they witness to them or not. The problem, however, in this kind of thinking is that they have failed to understand that God not only foreordains the end of salvation, but also the means to that end. Not only has God chosen to save particular persons; He has chosen to save them through the communication of the gospel. Far from causing us to cease evangelizing, this truth gives us the certainty that our efforts will be successful. If there were no such thing as election, there would be no converts and heaven would be empty. But since God has chosen a vast multitude that no man can number (Revelation 7:9), we can be absolutely sure that these chosen people will be brought into His kingdom. Knowing this causes God's people to burn with zeal to proclaim the gospel so that these chosen ones will be saved. Because Jesus was convinced that God had chosen a people, He could say in John 10:16, "I *have* other sheep, which are not of this fold; I *must* bring them also, and *they shall* hear My voice; and *they shall* become one flock with one shepherd." Far from quenching the fire of evangelism in Jesus' ministry, it caused Him to cry, "I *must* bring them also!"

The doctrine of election actually proved to be a great encouragement to the apostle Paul. While in Corinth, the Lord appeared to Paul in a vision and said, "Do not be afraid any longer, but go on speaking and do not be silent; for I am with you, and no man will attack you in order to harm you, *for I have many people in this city*" (Acts 18:9-10). In his commentary on this passage John Gill states:

> it is very likely that after the baptism of Crispus and his family, and of many of the Corinthians, that both the Jews and the Gentiles were exasperated against the apostle; and his life might seem to be in danger, and he might be thinking of removing from hence for his preservation and safety; and might be advised to it by his friends, or at least that he should be incognito, and not be seen publicly: wherefore the Lord appears to him, and bids him not indulge any fears, or conceal himself and be silent, *but speak, and hold not*

thy peace; preach freely and boldly the Gospel without fear of men.[3]

The Lord roused Paul to continue speaking by giving him a three-fold encouragement: 1) He would be with him; 2) He would protect Him; and 3) He had many people in that city. By virtue of God's electing grace, He had many people in Corinth that were His, even though they had not yet come to faith. This message so encouraged Paul, that he settled there a year and six months, teaching the word of God among them (Acts 18:11).

To further prove that this truth need not put out the fire of evangelism, simply look at church history to see that some of the most evangelistic preachers, pastors, and missionaries who have ever lived have believed the doctrines of sovereign grace including George Whitefield, Jonathan Edwards, William Carey, and Charles Spurgeon.

I can truthfully say that the truth of God's sovereign grace has not put out our zeal for evangelism, but rather has inflamed it. In the church I pastored, teams of believers would regularly go out and proclaim Christ on trains, buses, shopping malls, and outdoor events. Some of the young people wrote their own tracts and actively distributed them on college campuses to their classmates. Far from quenching our zeal for evangelism, the truths of sovereign grace have only stoked the fires, because they inform us that Christ has a people that He *must* bring, and they *will* come and be brought within His fold (John 10:16).

As we proclaim the glad tidings of salvation, we are confident that Christ will save His elect.

How Can You Know If You Are One Of God's Elect?

This is an absolutely crucial question! If in the end you are not among the number of God's chosen people, none of the glorious truths we have seen from Scripture apply to you. Be very careful that you do not assume you are one of God's elect, without sufficient warrant to do so. Jesus declared in Matthew 7:21-23, "Not everyone who says to Me, 'Lord, Lord,' will enter the kingdom of heaven, but he who does the will of My Father who is in heaven. Many will say to Me on that day, 'Lord, Lord, did we not prophesy in Your name, and in Your name cast out demons, and in Your name perform many miracles? And then I will declare to them, 'I never knew you; depart from Me, you who practice lawlessness.'" Notice that there will be *many* who will be shocked to find out that Christ never knew them - not just a few. What was their confidence in? They trusted in their profession of faith and spiritual gifts. They called Jesus "Lord." However, a verbal confession of Christ alone should never assure someone that they are of God's elect. They also prophesied, cast out demons, and worked miracles. However, none of these things are evidence of true conversion. According to Jesus, true conversion is evidenced by doing the will of the Father who is in heaven. While the non-elect practice lawless-ness, the elect are known by obedience to God.

What are some Biblical marks of a true child of God?

1. He has as his ambition to please the Lord (2 Corinthians 5:9)
2. He does not practice sin (1 John 3:9)
3. He practices righteousness (1 John 3:10)
4. He loves the brethren (1 John 3:14)
5. He believes that Jesus is the Christ (1 John 5:1)
6. He has been given a new heart and a new spirit (Ezekiel 36:26)
7. He is a new creation; old things have passed away and new things have come (2 Corinthians 5:17)
8. He has been made spiritually alive (Ephesians 2:5)
9. He loves the Lord (1 Corinthians 16:22)
10. He is indwelt by Jesus Christ (2 Corinthians 13:5)
11. He experiences the Spirit bearing witness with his spirit that he is a child of God (Romans 8:16)
12. He is disciplined by the Lord when he pursues sin (Hebrews 12:8)

Although these marks are by no means exhaus-tive, they will provide a good start in evaluating whether or not you are His child. Peter tells us to "be all the more diligent to make certain about His calling and choosing you" (2 Peter 1:10). In the preceding context, he tells us the way to know God has called and chosen you is to see growth in your life in the areas of faith, moral excellence, knowledge, self-control, perseverance, godliness, brotherly kindness, and love.

If after looking at the Biblical marks of conversion you are not sure that God has saved you, determine you will never rest until it becomes evident that you are His child. Instead of trusting in yourself that you are righteous, go to the Lord with a humble and repentant heart, cast yourself on His mercy, and cry out, "God, be merciful to me, the sinner" (Luke 18:9-14). Continue to do this, until you know that He has given you a new heart and put a new spirit within you. Then, for the rest of your life and throughout eternity, magnify and praise His sovereign grace which, alone, has made you to differ (1 Corinthians 4:7 KJV)!

NOTES:

1. Iain Murray, *The Forgotten Spurgeon,* (Carlisle, Pennsylvania: The Banner Of Truth Trust, 1966) footnotes 62.

2. Iain Murray, *Forgotten Spurgeon,* 62.

3. John Gill, *Exposition of the Old and New Testaments, Volume 8,* (Paris, Arkansas: The Baptist Standard Bearer, 1989) 317.

Chapter 10

Responding To Sovereign Grace

~~~

Now that we have seen how thrilling God's sovereign grace is, let us note in conclusion how we can respond to this grace in a way that will glorify Him.

Let God's Sovereign Grace Move You To Worship

At the conclusion of Paul's discussion of God's sovereign plan for Israel in Romans chapters nine, ten, and eleven, he bursts out in spontaneous praise, "Oh, the depth of the riches both of the wisdom and knowledge of God! How unsearchable are His judgments and unfathomable His ways! For 'Who has known the mind of the Lord, or who became His counselor? Or who has first given to Him that it might be paid back to him again?' For from Him and through Him and to Him are all things. To Him be the glory forever. Amen" (Romans 11:33-36). The truth of God's sovereign grace left the apostle Paul overwhelmed. All he can do is bow in the dust and give all the glory to his awe-inspiring God.

As we understand God's grace, it will have the same effect in our lives. We were rebels, running as fast as we could from God. We spurned His invitations and despised His Word. Yet, before we were even born, He had already purposed to set His saving love upon us. He sent His Son for the express purpose of dying for our sins. He sent His Spirit to make us alive when we were dead in sin and lying under the wrath of God. All of this came to us, not because we deserved it, but in spite of the fact that we deserved to spend eternity in hell. Oh, we need to let these truths press us to our knees in adoring wonder, love, and praise.

This is exactly what these truths did for the apostle Paul. As he considered God's sovereign grace in election, it caused him to burst forth in praise, "Blessed be the God and Father of our Lord Jesus Christ, who has blessed us with every spiritual blessing in the heavenly places in Christ, just as He chose us in Him before the foundation of the world, that we should be holy and blameless before Him. In love He predestined us to adoption as sons through Jesus Christ to Himself, according to the kind intention of His will, to the praise of the glory of His grace, which He freely bestowed on us in the Beloved" (Ephesians 1:3-6).

Isaac Watts, the great hymn writer, has captured the kind of praise God's sovereign love should evoke from our lives in these lines:

> Jesus, we bless thy Father's name;
> Thy God and ours are both the same,
> What heavenly blessings from his throne
> Flow down to sinners through his Son!

> "Christ be my first elect," he said;
> Then chose our souls in Christ, our Head,
> Before he gave the mountains birth,
> Or laid foundations for the earth.

> Thus did eternal love begin
> To raise us up from death and sin;
> Our characters were then decreed,
> Blameless in love, a holy seed.

> Predestinated to be sons,
> Born by degrees, but chose at once;
> A new regenerated race,
> to praise the glory of his grace.[1]

Let God's Sovereign Grace Move You To Humility

When you realize that your salvation is all of God, your perspective begins to change. No longer will you chalk up your Christian faith to the fact that you had the sense to exercise your free will and believe in Christ when so many others around you went on persistently in their sins. You realize now that if God had left you to your free will, it would have taken you straight to hell. No, the fact that you are a Christian today has nothing to do with you, and everything to do with Him. God's sovereign grace laid hold of you when you had no love for Him. Before reading this book you may have thought, "Yes, God gave me salvation, but I received it. He offered it to all, but not everybody was smart enough to take Him up on it." If that were true, you could stand up in heaven, look down on the man in hell and say, "Look buddy, you are there because you didn't do what I did, plain and simple." But the sovereign grace of God removes all possibility for boasting. Now the only thing you can boast in is the cross of our Lord Jesus Christ. "But may it never be that I should boast, except in the cross of our Lord Jesus Christ, through which the world has been crucified to me, and I to the world" (Galatians 6:14). Through the grace of God you are what you are (1 Corinthians 15:10)! Let him who boasts, boast in the Lord (1 Corinthians 1:31).

Let God's Sovereign Grace Move You To Obedience

Could there be a more compelling truth to move us to obedience? Paul declares, "And so, as those who have been *chosen of God*, holy and beloved, put on a heart of compassion, kindness, humility, gentleness and patience" (Colossians 3:12). Spurgeon declared:

Nothing under the gracious influence of the Holy Spirit can make a Christian more holy than the thought that He is chosen. Shall I sin after God has chosen me? Shall I transgress after such love? Shall I go astray after so much lovingkindness and tender mercy? No, my God, since Thou hast chosen me, I will love Thee, I will live to Thee, I will give myself to Thee to be Thine forever, solemnly consecrating myself to Thy service forever.[2]

Oh, go on to bring much glory to our great God who loved us with an everlasting love. Let us seek to do great exploits in His strength. Let us seek to bring honor and praise to One so deserving, so worthy, so glorious. Let us love supremely the One who first loved us!

Let God's Sovereign Grace Move You To Face The Future With Confidence

What confidence in the future can a person possess whose salvation is a result of his own initiative? If I believe my free will is what got me into a state of salvation, then I must believe that it can also get me out as well. In that case, I would have to trust in myself, at least to some degree, to persevere to the end. Now, that is a scary thought. There is no comfort there at all. No wonder the framers of the 39 Articles of the Church of England wrote, "The godly consideration of predestination and our election in Christ is full of sweet, pleasant, and unspeakable comfort to godly persons."[3]

Oh, it is indeed. Go on trusting Him. If He began this work of grace, He will perfect it until the day of Christ Jesus (Philippians 1:6). Find your confidence and security in Him and His work on your behalf. The more confident we are in Him, the more glory we will bring to Him.

NOTES:

1. William Gadsby, *A Selection of Hymns for Public Worship*, (Herts, England: The Gospel Standard Societies, 1991) 69.

2. Taken from one of John MacArthur, Jr.'s sermon tapes on 1 Peter 1:1-2 entitled, *Chosen By God.*

3. Philip Schaff, *Creeds, Vol. 3*, 498.

Suggestions For Further Reading

~~~

Belcher, Richard P., *A Journey In Grace*, (Columbia, South Carolina: Richbarry Press) 1990.

Berkhof, Louis, *Systematic Theology*, (Grand Rapids, Michigan: William B. Eerdmans Publishing Company) 1939.

Boettner, Loraine, *The Reformed Doctrine Of Predestination*, (Phillipsburg, New Jersey: Presbyterian & Reformed Publishing Company) 1932.

Boice, James Montgomery and Ryken, Philip Graham, *The Doctrines of Grace: Rediscovering the Evangelical Gospel*, (Wheaton, Illinois: Crossway Books) 2002.

Gill, John, *A Body Of Doctrinal And Practical Divinity,* (Paris, Arkansas: The Baptist Standard Bearer) 1989.

Gill, John, *The Cause Of God And Truth,* (Paris, Arkansas: The Baptist Standard Bearer) 1992.

Grudem, Wayne, *Systematic Theology,* (Grand Rapids, Michigan: Zondervan) 1994.

Hoekema, Anthony A., *Saved By Grace*, (Grand Rapids, Michigan: William B. Eerdmans Publishing Company) 1989.

Horton, Michael Scott, *Putting Amazing Back Into Grace*, (Nashville, Tennessee: Thomas Nelson Publishers) 1991.

Murray, Iain, *The Forgotten Spurgeon*, (Carlisle, Pennsylvania: Banner Of Truth Trust) 1966.

Murray, John, *Redemption Accomplished And Applied*, (Grand Rapids, Michigan: William B. Eerdmans Publishing Company) 1955.

Owen, John, *The Death Of Death In The Death Of Christ,* (Carlisle, Pennsylvania: Banner Of Truth Trust) 1959.

Phillips, Richard D., *What's So Great About The Doctrines Of Grace,* (Orlando, Florida: Ligonier Ministries) 2008.

Pink, Arthur W., *The Sovereignty Of God*, (Carlisle, Pennsylvania: Banner Of Truth Trust) 1928.

Pink, Arthur W., *The Attributes Of God*, (Grand Rapids, Michigan: Baker Book House) 1975.

Piper, John, *The Justification of God,* (Grand Rapids, Michigan: Baker Book House) 1993.

Sproul, R. C., *Chosen By God*, (Wheaton, Illinois: Tyndale House Publishers) 1986.

Sproul, R. C., *What Is Reformed Theology?: Understanding The Basics,* (Grand Rapids, Michigan: Baker Book House) 2005.

Steele, David N. & Thomas, Curtis C., *The Five Points Of Calvinism*, (Phillipsburg, New Jersey: Presbyterian & Reformed Publishing Company) 1963.

Wells, Tom, *A Price For A People*, (Carlisle, Pennsylvania: Banner Of Truth Trust) 1992.

James R. White, *The Potter's Freedom: A Defense of the Reformation and the Rebuttal of Norman Geisler's Chosen But Free,* (Amityville, New York: Calvary Press Publishing) 2000.

Zanchius, Jerome, *Absolute Predestination,* (Jenkintown, Pennsylvania: Sovereign Grace Publishers) n.d.